CLIP aRT cRaZy

Windows Edition

*If you appreciate terrific illustration, if you love
creative ideas, if you want to know how to find clip art,
choose it, and use it, you're about to go . . .*

CLip aRT cRaZy

Windows Edition

*Includes the Clip Art Crazy CD-ROM featuring
500 clip art images by some of the world's top illustrators*

Chuck Green

Peachpit Press

Clip Art Crazy

Chuck Green

Peachpit Press
2414 Sixth Street
Berkeley, CA 94710 USA
Voice: 510/548-4393
Fax: 510/548-5991

Find us on the World Wide Web at: http://www.peachpit.com

Peachpit Press is a division of Addison-Wesley Publishing Company

Edited by Jeremy Judson
Copyedited by Tema Goodwin
Design by Chuck Green
Cover by TMA, Ted Mader Associates

Notice of Rights

Notice of Liability

ISBN 0-201-88361-9

9 8 7 6 5 4 3 2 1

Printed and Bound in the United States of America

Dedication

To my wife Leslie and sons Jeffrey and Robert.

Computer–from the Task Force Clip Art, Home Edition. © 1995 New Vision Technologies Inc. All rights reserved.

Acknowledgments

A heartfelt thank you to all the talented illustrators who created these images and to the companies that had the insight to publish them. Each and every image represents countless ideas launched and abandoned and untold hours of production, refinement, product development, and marketing. Hard work with extraordinary results.

Thanks to Charlie and Leslie Clark for their input on the book design, to Mike Damrath for his technical help, to Dennis McWaters for his splendid photography, to Charlie Green for his woodworking on the Stencil project, to Jeff Heinz for his packaging expertise, and to the professionals of Peachpit Press; Ted Nace, Jeremy Judson, and Tema Goodwin for their ideas, support, and counsel.

Table of Contents

Compass rose-from Volume 7-Circular Designs of Design Elements. © 1995 Ultimate Symbol Inc. All rights reserved.

Opposite: Paperwork–from the Workplace category of Megatoons Part II. © 1995 Creative Media Services. All rights reserved.

x

Introduction Forget everything you've heard about "clip art" —it's time to rewrite the definition.

The original idea was simple—the artist created an illustration, printed up copies, and sold it to the trade en masse. The buyer "clipped" the illustration from the sheet, pasted it onto their advertisement or newsletter, and sent it off to be printed.

Unfortunately, the cut and paste medium not only limited the artist to simple line drawings, but generic concepts were also often weak concepts, and the quality of the illustration was spotty.

But times have changed. With the evolution of computer hardware and software, techniques that were not practical a few years ago—color, even delicate pencil drawings and photographic images—can be created and distributed electronically. The explosive growth of the desktop publishing audience and the resulting market for packaged images is attracting artists who are routinely paid hundreds or thousands of dollars to create a single illustration.

Improved quality and better-focused results are attracting the high-end publishers, ad agencies, and design studios that

once shunned canned art. And as the print, multimedia, and online publishing fields expand, so will the need for the talents of people who can translate ideas into visual form. Negative momentum turns positive. Call it what you like—illustrations, images, pictures—clip art is real art.

xii

Face–from the Faces set. © 1995 Art Parts. All rights reserved.

Pinch Me, I Think I'm Dreamin'

For a clip art nut, putting this book together was more fun than work. On the pages that follow, I'll show you the work of many talented artists and demonstrate ways to incorporate their images into your designs.

You'll meet The Oswego Company, a group of artists whose illustrations are so precise that at first glance you'd swear they were photographs. And Iconomics, a cooperative of illustrators who are offering an interesting new alternative for purchasing stock and custom artwork. Individuals such as Daniel Pelavin, an award-winning illustrator who is offering a collection of his spot illustrations for the first time. And partners Ron and Joe of Art Parts, the only guys I know who use a beanie as part of their strategic marketing plan.

But what you see and read here is just the beginning. The *Clip Art Crazy CD-ROM* includes 25 images from each of 20 stellar clip art sources. I have had the envious job of searching through tens of thousands of images to select 500 that, in my opinion, demonstrate the width and breadth of the available subjects and styles. They form a base from which you can decide what to buy from whom. Because, believe me, once you've sampled the best, you're going to want more.

xiii

What You Need

The beauty of electronic clip art is that virtually every desktop publishing, word processing, and presentation software package has the tools to import, size, and crop it. Graphics software gives you the power to edit it. And both laser and graphics printers will print it. All you need is a CD-ROM drive attached to your computer and you're ready for liftoff.

Juggler–from Publisher's Task Force, Volume 1. © 1995 New Vision Technologies Inc. All rights reserved.

How to Use This Book

Clip Art Crazy is divided into three parts. PART I, the Clip Art Basics, will get you oriented:

Surprise–from the Journeys font from Fontek DesignFonts. © 1995 Letraset USA. All rights reserved.

Chapter 1 • Find It, briefly profiles and provides the names, addresses, and phone numbers of more than 100 clip art sources—a map you can use to hunt for more treasure.

Once you've found it, Chapter 2 • Choose It, will help you determine the style of image that best suits your project and help you separate the good from the not so good.

Chapter 3 • Use It, maps out the technical terrain— the file formats that best suit your system, clip art effects you can re-create, and some things you need to know about using copyrighted art.

Most often, when people think about clip art, a few tried and true projects come to mind—brochures and newsletters for example. In PART II, Clip Art Projects, I'll show you 50 design projects that break the mold—everything from stencils, calendars, and posters to multimedia presentations, "cake stakes," and clocks that are worth watching—each with a how-to description and a photograph.

PART III of *Clip Art Crazy,* the Clip Art Catalog, profiles 20 of my favorite clip art sources. Companies that demonstrate the innovations that have redefined the business.

Each company has its own chapter with tidbits about the people behind the pictures and a catalog of the illustrations they have contributed to the *Clip Art Crazy CD-ROM*. Later, these chapters serve as a quick reference for finding just the right image.

In the Appendix you'll find information from all 20 companies along with coupons you can use to purchase the complete libraries from which the samples are taken.

How To Use the CD-ROM

The *Clip Art Crazy CD-ROM* is enclosed in a pouch on the inside back cover of this book. It includes over 500 clip art images and other graphics goodies. Instructions for using the CD-ROM begin on page 356.

Computer–from Designer's Club. © 1995 Dynamic Graphics Inc. All rights reserved.

I'd Like to Hear From You

I'm eager to get your feedback and to hear about new clip art, photo, and font sources. I encourage you to return the survey on page 358 or if you'd prefer, send your comments to:

Chuck Green, P.O. Box 3192, Glen Allen, Virginia 23058

CompuServe: 70611,1370

Internet: 70611.1370@compuserve.com

The New Definition

The new definition for clip art includes quality, creativity, and technical excellence. If you haven't tried it, this is a great place to start. If you're already choosing and using clip art, this book will open a new universe of ideas and sources. If I've done my job, you'll come away with a new appreciation for illustration and the folks who create it, and a clear understanding of what it really means to be *Clip Art Crazy.*

Chuck Green

Glen Allen, Virginia

Part I

Clip Art Basics

1

2

Chapter 1

Find It

Find It Begin your hunt with a map.

Pictures are treasure—gold, silver, precious stones, and the inevitable baubles. They are ideas personified. If you can imagine the number of illustrations people have put to paper in even the last 100 years, you begin to appreciate the scope of the treasure to be found.

But finding treasure is seldom easy. This book provides a considerable core of styles and content from which to choose, but there is much more to be had.

Like artists, clip art companies are an unconventional bunch. Each is determined to plot its own unique course. Some choose a subject niche—BBL Typographic, for example, publishes collections based on medieval, Renaissance, and Greek art. Tech-M provides highly detailed drawings of computer parts, mechanical fasteners, network symbols, etc., for technical publishing. Judith Sutcliffe: The Electric Typographer, crafts pictographs in font form.

Others generate art for the full spectrum of business and personal publishing. Subscribe to Dynamic Graphics' Electronic Clipper and you'll receive a broad range of general and seasonal images every month of the year. New Vision Technologies' Task Force collection includes people, cartoons, food, music, nature, and more in a single collection.

The purpose of pictures runs the gamut, too. Art Beats has a gift for decorative borders and backgrounds. And Ultimate Symbol publishes a CD-ROM filled with beautifully simple symbols, icons, and ornaments.

You'll discover all manner of graphics delivered in conventional cut and paste form, as individual files in an assortment of electronic flavors, or as computer fonts that allow you to type pictures instead of letters.

4

How to Use the Source List

So you begin the hunt with a map. With it you'll find all kinds of sources and the promise of all kinds of treasure.

Twenty of the companies listed here are profiled in detail beginning on page 159. I've chosen them for the quality of their artwork, their diversity of style, and their technical skill. You'll find 25 samples from each of the 20 on the *Clip Art Crazy CD-ROM* and coupons for purchasing their complete libraries in the appendix beginning on page 325.

But they're just the tip of the iceberg. Many of the other sources listed are every bit as impressive as the 20 profiled here. All have individual images that are worth a look.

Noticeably absent are companies that include clip art as part of their products—there simply wasn't space. And I've bypassed companies that sell art by the pound—50,000 high-quality images for $19.95—as I believe you get what you pay for.

All of the artwork used to illustrate *Clip Art Crazy* is credited to one of the sources listed here. If you see an image you like, check the credit located beside, above, or below it. You'll find that some of the images are located on the CD-ROM; the others you can order directly from the source.

The descriptions are necessarily brief: just company and product names, contact information, and a summary that lists a representative sample of subject titles. As you can imagine, most of the sources remain in constant motion creating new work and branching out with new styles and subject matter. Whether you call, write, or explore through the Internet, you are certain to uncover a fortune in visual ideas.

Treasure chest–from Presentation Task Force, Volume 4. © 1995 New Vision Technologies Inc. All rights reserved.

5

Jazz trio–from the People 1 set. © 1995 3G Graphics Inc. All rights reserved.

Clip Art Source List

3G Graphics Inc.
Images With Impact!
114 Second Ave. South #104, Edmonds, WA 98020 USA
Voice: 800-456-0234, 206-774-3518; Fax: 206-771-8975
Images for the PC and Macintosh. Subjects include Business, Health, Cartoons & Fun, Sports, Presentation Helpers, and others.

Adobe Systems Inc.
Clip art fonts
1585 Charleston Rd., Mountain View, CA 94039-7900 USA
Voice: 800-445-8787, 415-962-2798; Fax: 415-962-2659
Clip art fonts for the PC and Macintosh. Subjects include Giddyyup Thangs, Wood Type Ornaments, Carta, Poetica Ornaments, Caslon Ornaments, and others.

AfroLink Software
CPTime Clip Art
P.O. Box 36708, Los Angeles, CA 90036-0708
Voice: 800-442-3765, 213-731-5465; Fax: 213-730-0653
Images for the PC and Macintosh. Subjects include African, African American, Afri-Caribbean leaders, ancient symbols, Black memorabilia, and others.

After Images Company
Western Clip Art Pack
P.O. Box 4803, Cave Creek, AZ 85331 USA
Voice: 800-278-7225
Images for the PC and Macintosh. Subjects include old west themes.

Agfa Division, Miles Inc.
Clip Art Fonts
200 Ballardvale St., Wilmington, MA 01887 USA
Voice: 800-424-8973, 508-658-5600; Fax: 508-657-8568
Clip art fonts for the PC and Macintosh. Subjects include Petroglyph, Maskerade, Electric Stamps, FinFont, Easter Island, and others.

Allegro New Media Inc.
InPrint Art Library
16 Passaic Ave., Bldg 6, Fairfield, NJ 07004 USA
Voice: 800-424-1992, 201-808-1992; Fax: 201-808-2645

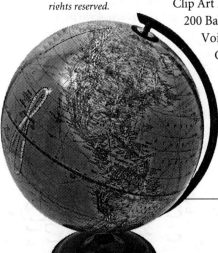

Globe–from the Graphic Photos CD-ROM. © 1995 Allegro New Media Inc. All rights reserved.

6

Images for the PC and Macintosh. Subjects include Frames, Hands, Trophies, Celebrations, and others.

Alpha Media

MediClip
P.O. Box 1719, Maryland Heights, MO 63043 USA
Voice: 314-692-2329; Fax: 314-692-2031
Images for the PC and Macintosh. Medical subjects include Anatomy, Medical Art, Instruments, and others.

Alphabets Inc.

Clip Art Fonts
P.O. Box 5448, Evanston, IL 60204 USA
Voice: 800-326-8973, 708-328-2733; Fax: 708-328-1922,
Internet: http://www.dol.com/ or info@alphabets.com
Clip art fonts for the PC and Macintosh. Subjects include Before the Alphabet, Flighty, AppleWine, UniTronica, Tours and Travels, and others.

Altemus Creative Servicenter

The Altemus Collection
613 East 6th St. #5B, New York, NY 10009 USA
Voice: 212-529-7102; Fax: 212-529-7103
Clip art fonts for the PC and Macintosh. Subjects include graphic symbols, devices, decorative icons, and others.

Aridi Computer Graphics Inc.

Aridi Art Images
P.O. Box 797702, Dallas, TX 75379 USA
Voice: 800-755-6441, 214-404-9171; Fax: 214-404-9172
Featured in Chapter 6. See the Appendix for a special offer from Aridi Computer Graphics. Images for the PC and Macintosh. Subjects include Initial Caps, Historical Ornaments, Arabesque Ornaments & Borders, Olde World Borders, and others.

ARISEN Corporation (formally Arro International)

ARROglyphs
P.O. Box 969, Milford, PA 18337 USA
Voice: 800-243-1515 ext. 485, 717-296-5490; Fax: 717-296-5491
Featured in Chapter 7. See the Appendix for a special offer from Arro International. Images for the PC and Macintosh. Subjects include Energy, Wildlife, Living Planet, Recycling, Pollution, and others.

Walking–from the A*I HeShelt font. © 1995 Alphabets Inc. All rights reserved.

Initial capital–from Volume 7-Initial Caps III-Victoriana font. © 1995 Aridi Computer Graphics Inc. All rights reserved.

Forest fire–from the Living Planet volume. © 1995 ARISEN Corp. All rights reserved.

7

8

Art Direction Book Company

Book/Disk Series

10 East 39th St., New York, NY 10016 USA

Voice: 212-889-6500; Fax: 212-889-6504

Images in book and disk form for the PC and Macintosh. Titles include Mostly Happy Clip Art 2 of the 30s, 40s, 50s, Borders 5, 101 Absolutely Superb Icons; and others.

Art Parts

Art Parts

P.O. Box 2926, Orange, CA 92669-0926 USA

Voice: 714-771-6754; Fax: 714-633-9617

Featured in Chapter 8. See the Appendix for a special offer from Art Parts. Images for the PC and Macintosh. Subjects include Finance, Relations, Occupations, Home & Family, Entertainment, and others.

ARTBEATS

ARTBEATS

P.O. Box 709, Myrtle Creek, OR 97457

Voice: 800-444-9392, 541-863-4429; Fax: 541-863-4547

Background images for the PC and Macintosh. Subjects include grids, patterns, textures, natural images, and others.

Art Maker Company

Art Maker Disk Art Library

1420 N. Claremont Blvd. #205-D, Claremont, CA 91711 USA

Voice: 800-434-7527, 909-626-8065; Fax: 909-621-1323

Images for the PC and Macintosh. Subjects include Wealth, Meat & Poultry, Springtime, Famous Places, High Tech, and others.

AUTOLOGIC Inc.

Clip Art Fonts

1050 Rancho Conejo Blvd., Thousand Oaks, CA 91320-1794 USA

Voice: 800-457-8973, 805-498-9611; Fax: 805-498-7099

Clip art fonts for the PC and Macintosh. Subjects include Fancy Borders, Newspaper Pi, TV Logos, and others.

Baudville Desktop Publishing Solutions

Award Clips

5380 52nd St. S.E., Grand Rapids, MI 49512 USA

Voice: 800-728-0888; Fax: 616-698-0554

Images for the PC and Macintosh. Subjects include business, motivation, music, sports, religion, and others.

BBL Typographic

Medieval and Renaissance Clip Art Library
137 Narrow Neck Rd., Katoomba, NSW 2780, Australia
Voice: 011-61-47-82-6111; Fax: 011-61-47-82-6144,
Internet: bblart@acslink.net.au
Images for the PC and Macintosh. Subjects include Ancient Greece,
Middle Ages & Renaissance, and others.

*Woman–from the Ancient
Greek I, II, & III sets.*

Broderbund Software Inc.

Print Shop Deluxe Clip Art
P.O. Box 6125, Novato, CA 94948-6125 USA
Voice: 800-521-6263
Images for the PC and Macintosh. Subjects include Carmen Sandiego,
Business, Sports, People at Work, Comic Characters, and others.

C.A.R. Inc.

CLIPables
4661 Maryland Ave. #200, St. Louis, MO 63108 USA
Voice: 800-288-7585, 314-721-6305; Fax: 314-454-0105
Images for the PC and Macintosh. Subjects include Travel, Dingbats,
Business, Humor, Maps, Sports, and others.

Caddylak Systems, Inc

Art Portfolios
510 Fillmore Ave., Tonawanda, NY 14150 USA
Voice: 800-523-8060; Fax: 800-222-1934
Images in book form. Titles include Bar, Pie, and Percentage Graphs;
Borders; Holiday & Special Occasion; Motivation & Achievement; and
others.

Cartesia Software

MapArt
5 South Main St., Lambertville, NJ 08530 USA
Voice: 800-334-4291; Fax: 609-397-5724
Images for the PC and Macintosh. Subjects include Designer Series
World & USA, Clip Art Pack, and others.

Castle Systems

Clip Art Fonts
1306 Lincoln Ave., San Rafael, CA 94901-2105 USA
Voice: 415-459-6495; Fax: 415-459-6495
Clip art fonts for the PC and Macintosh. Subjects include Afrika
Ornaments, Afrika Borders, Castle Fleurons, and others.

Crow–from Megatoons II.

Books–from Church Art Plus On Disk.

Cat–from the CSA Archive.

Creative Media Services (CMS)

Megatoons

P.O. Box 5955, Berkeley, CA 94705 USA

Voice: 800-358-2278, 510-843-3408; Fax: 510-549-2490

Featured in Chapter 9. See the Appendix for a special offer from CMS. Images for the PC and Macintosh. Subjects include Awards, Business, Education, Political, Workplace, and others.

Communication Resources Inc.

Church Art Plus On Disk

4150 Belden Village St., Canton, OH 44718 USA

Voice: 800-992-2144; Fax: 216-493-7897,

Internet: 73144.3650@compuserve.com

Subscription service for the PC and Macintosh. Christian subjects include Church Events, Missions, Meals, Youth Activities, Sunday School, and others.

Communications Shop

Just Dingbats

247 N. Goodman St., Rochester, NY 14607 USA

Voice: 800-733-1650, 716-473-1650; Fax: 716-473-5201

Clip art fonts for the PC and Macintosh. Subjects include Healthcare, American Politics, Signs & Symbols, Christian Symbols, DingDongs, and others.

Computer A.D.vantage

Clip Art Volumes

P.O. Box 2329, Camarillo, CA 93011 USA

Voice: 805-485-2688

Images for the PC and Macintosh. Subjects include Aliens, Sports, Animals, Cartoons, and others.

CSA Archive Company

CSA Archive Diskette Collection & CD Sampler

P.O. Box 581639, Minneapolis, MN 55458-1639 USA

Voice: 612-339-1263; Fax: 612-339-3283,

Internet: http://www.csa-archive.com

Featured in Chapter 10. See the Appendix for a special offer from The CSA Archive Company. Images for the PC and Macintosh. CD-ROM collection and a huge collection of stock illustrations sold on a per-image basis.

Davka Corp.

DavkaGraphics Deluxe Series

7074 N. Western Ave., Chicago, IL 60645 USA

Voice: 800-621-8227; Fax: 312-262-9298,

Internet: vo185@applelink.apple.com

Clip art fonts and images for the PC and Macintosh. Subjects include Judaica, Israel & Holidays, Special Occasions, and DavkaBats Font.

Decathlon Corp.

Logo SuperPower and Instant Logos

4100 Executive Park Dr. #16, Cincinnati, OH 45241 USA

Voice: 800-648-5646, 513-421-1938; Fax: 606-324-6038 (orders only)

Images for the PC and Macintosh. Subjects include Southwestern, Woodcuts, Pictographs, a graphic database of design elements, and others.

Baseball–from Instant Logos. © 1995 Decathlon Corp. All rights reserved.

DENIART Systems

Clip Art Fonts

Box 1074, Adelaide Stn., Toronto, Ontario, Canada M5C 2K5

Voice: 416-941-0919; Fax: 416-941-0948

Clip art fonts for the PC and Macintosh. Subjects include Egyptian Hieroglyphics, Alchemy Symbols, Signals & Signs, Castles & Shields, and others.

Design OnLine Inc.

Design OnLine

2490 Black Rock Turnpike #339, Fairfield, CT 06430 USA

Voice: 203-330-1600; Fax: 203-330-1225

Membership service and custom illustration for the PC and Macintosh. Subjects include Workplace, Beasts/Bugs/Bountiful Sea, Ethnic, Home Sweet Home, Technology/Communications, and others.

Crown–from the Judaica set. © 1995 Davka Corp. All rights reserved.

Design Plus

Design Plus and Graphic Designer Tools

853 Broadway #1607, New York, NY 10003 USA

Voice: 800-231-3461, 212-477-8811

Fonts and images for the PC and Macintosh. Subjects include Icons, Kinetic Patterns, Stencils, Intaglios, Breaks, and others.

12

Digital Knowledge Corp.

ELECTRICIris

6217 Edgemont Blvd. Suite B, Minneapolis, MN 55428 USA

Voice: 800-279-6099, 612-531-9811; Fax: 612-531-9812

Images for the PC and Macintosh. Subjects include backgrounds, design elements, and others.

Digital Media

Stock Options

28382 Via Nandina, Laguna Niguel, CA 92656 USA

Voice: 800-786-2512, 714-362-5103; Fax: 714-643-2426

Photo clip art for the PC and Macintosh. Subjects include Sports Equipment, Food & Grocery Items, Toys, Models & Game Pieces, Business & Medical Items, and others.

Digital Wisdom Inc.

Mountain High Maps

P.O. Box 2070, Tappahannock, VA 22560 USA

Voice: 800-800-8560, 804-758-0670; Fax: 804-758-4512

Images for the PC and Macintosh. Subjects include highly detailed maps and globes.

Dover Publications

Ready-To-Use Series

31 East 2nd St., Mineola, NY 11501 USA

Voice: Mail orders only

Images in book form. Titles in the Ready-To-Use series include School & Education Illustrations, Wedding Illustrations, Wining & Dining Illustrations, Office & Business Illustrations, Old-Fashioned Romantic Cuts, and others.

Dream Maker Software

MacGallery and Cliptures

925 W Kenyon Ave. #16, Englewood, CO 80110 USA

Voice: 800-876-5665, 303-762-1001; Fax: 303-762-0762,

Internet: dreammaker@eworld.com, eWorld: DreamMaker

Images for the PC and Macintosh. Subjects include Holidays & Special Occasions, Business Cartoons, Business Images, 19th Century Accents, World Flags, and others.

DS Design

KidBAG

1157 Executive Circle Suite D, Cary, NC 27511 USA

Voice: 800-745-4037, 919-319-1770; Fax: 919-460-5983

Images and clip art fonts designed by children for the PC and Macintosh. Subjects include KidTYPE, Art By Kids, DingBRATS, FunTYPE, Woodcuts by Kids, and others.

Dubl-Click Software

WetPaint Clip Art

20310 Empire Ave. Suite A102, Bend, OR 97701-5713 USA

Voice: 800-359-9079, 503-317-0355; Fax: 503-317-0430,

Internet: dublclicks@aol.com

Images for the PC and Macintosh. Subjects include Island Life, Old Earth Almanac, Printer's Helper, Industrial Revolution, Pro Glyph, and others.

Bird–from WetSet CD-ROM. © 1995 Dubl-Click Software Inc. All rights reserved.

Dynamic Graphics Inc. (subscription services)

Designer's Club, Electronic Clipper,

Electronic Media Service, and Volk Clip Art

6000 N. Forest Park Dr., Peoria, IL 61656-3592 USA

Voice: 800-255-8800, 309-688-8800; Fax: 309-688-5873

Featured in Chapter 11. See the Appendix for a special offer from Dynamic Graphics. Subscription services for the PC and Macintosh. Subjects include corporate, retail, manufacturing, religious, backgrounds, and others.

Dynamic Graphics Inc. (packaged products)

ArtWorks

6000 N. Forest Park Dr., Peoria, IL 61656-3592 USA

Voice: 800-255-8800, 309-688-8800; Fax: 309-688-5873

Featured in Chapter 11. See the Appendix for a special offer from Dynamic Graphics. Packaged products for the PC and Macintosh. Categories include Showcase Series, PhotoConcepts Series, Encore Series, ArtAbout, Idea Source, and others.

EDUCORP

Clip Art Images

7434 Trade St., San Diego, CA 92121-2410

Voice: 800-843-9497, 619-536-9999

Images for the PC and Macintosh. Subjects include cartoons, backgrounds, design elements, and others.

13

Office workers–from the Electronic Clipper Service. © 1995 Dynamic Graphics Inc. All rights reserved.

14

ELDAR Company

Selective Ornaments

95 Liberty St., #A8, Stamford, CT 06902 USA

Voice: 203-359-3396; Fax: 203-359-2474

Images for the PC and Macintosh. Subjects include Asian, European, and Middle Eastern ornaments, motifs. textures, and backgrounds.

Emigre

Clip Art Fonts

4475 D St., Sacramento, CA 95819 USA

Voice: 800-944-9021, 916-451-4344; Fax: 916-451-4351

Clip art fonts for the PC and Macintosh. Subjects include FellaParts, Big Cheese, Whirligig, Zeitguys, and others.

Font Bureau

Clip Art Fonts

175 Newbury St., Boston, MA 02116 USA

Voice: 617-423-8770; Fax: 617-423-8771

Clip art fonts for the PC and Macintosh. Subjects include Interstate Pi, City Ornaments, Town Ornaments, Village Ornaments, and others.

FontHaus Inc.

Clip Art Fonts

1375 Kings Highway East, Fairfield, CT 06430 USA

Voice: 800-942-9110, 203-367-1993; Fax: 203-367-1860

Featured along with MvB Design in Chapter 17. See the Appendix for a special offer from MvB Design and FontHaus. Clip art fonts for the PC and Macintosh. Reseller for many of the small type foundries. Subjects include Bingo, Things, Isometric, Indian Summer, Damned Dingbats, and others.

FontShop USA Inc.

Clip Art Fonts

47 W. Polk St. #100-310, Chicago, IL 60605 USA

Voice: 800-897-3872, 416-593-4318; Fax: 312-360-1997

Clip art fonts for the PC and Macintosh. Subjects include Elementary Icons, Kosmik Glyphs, Mambo Initials, Tag Team Icons, Rian's Dingbats, and others.

General Glyphics

BorderFonts

3322 Shorecrest Dr. #100, Dallas, TX 75235 USA

Voice: 800-854-4061, 214-350-0952; Fax: 214-357-9843

Clip art fonts for the PC and Macintosh. Subjects include symbols used to create borders.

Graphic Products Corp.

Creative Gallery

1480 S. Wolf Rd., Wheeling, IL 60090-6514 USA

Voice: 800-323-1658, 708-537-9300; Fax: 708-215-0111

Images in disk and book form. Subjects include Business, Frontier Days, Graphic & Pictorial, Occupations, Monthly Events, and others.

Handcraftedfonts Company

Clip Art Fonts

P.O. Box 14013, Philadelphia, PA 19122 USA

Voice: 215-925-4457; Fax: 215-925-4457

Clip art fonts for the PC and Macintosh. Subjects include EdoFont Japanese Creats, Frankenfont figures, American Diner, and other fonts that include illustrated extended characters sets.

Harter Image Archives

Archive CD-ROM

4139 Gardendale St. #207, San Antonio, TX 78229 USA

Voice: 210-614-5942; Fax: 210-614-5922

Featured in Chapter 12. See the Appendix for a special offer from Harter Image Archives. Images for the PC and Macintosh. Subjects include Furniture, Men & Women, Law & Order, Insects, Tools & Implements, and others.

Heritage Graphics

Source I, II, and III Collections

P.O. Box 139, Blauvelt, NY 10913 USA

Voice: 914-359-0761

Images for the PC and Macintosh. Subjects include Judaic holidays, foods, symbols, traditions, and others.

Iconomics

Iconomics Stock and Custom Images

155 N. College Ave., Fort Collins, CO 80524 USA

Voice: 800-297-7658; Fax: 303-493-6997,

Internet: http://www.iconomics.com; E-mail: hipistrip@aol.com

Featured in Chapter 13. See the Appendix for a special offer from Iconomics. On-disk collection or stock illustrations sold on a per-image basis for the PC and Macintosh. Plus over 20 different illustrators creating custom images for specific projects.

Saxophone–from Assorted Images Volume 1. © 1995 Harter Image Archives. All rights reserved.

Star of David–from the Source collection. © 1995 Heritage Graphics. All rights reserved.

Birdbath–by Brian Jensen from Iconomics Stock and Custom Images. © 1995 Iconomics. All rights reserved.

16

Image Club Graphics Inc.

DigitArt

10545 West Donges Ct., Milwaukee, WI 53224-9985

Voice: 800-661-9410 (orders), 800-387-9193 (catalog requests);

Fax: 403-261-7013, Internet: http://www.adobe.com/imageclub/

Featured in Chapter 14. See the Appendix for a special offer from Image Club. Images for the PC and Macintosh. Subjects include Design Elements, Silhouettes, Fabulous Fifties, Science & Medicine, Art Jam, and others.

IMAGETECTS

ImageCELs

7200 Bollinger Rd. #802, San Jose, CA 95129 USA

Voice: 408-252-5487; Fax: 408-252-7409,

Internet: imagetects@aol.com

Photorealistic textures and images for the PC and Macintosh. Architectural and landscaping subjects include building materials, industrial finishes, people & vehicles, designer patterns, landscaping materials, and others.

IMAGINE THAT! Publications

FashionFindings and custom illustration

12200 Marion Lane #5120, Minnetonka, MN 55305

Voice: 800-843-6670, 612-593-9085; Fax: 612-544-6330

Fashion industry images for the PC and Macintosh. Subjects include Fabrics & Trimmings, Silhouettes (apparel), and others

IMSI

Masterclips

1895 E. Francisco Blvd., San Rafael, CA 94901 USA

Voice: 800-833-8082; Fax: 415-454-8901

Images for the PC and Macintosh. Subjects include Maps, Currencies, Flags, Landmarks, Holidays, and others.

Innovation Advertising & Design

AdArt

41 Mansfield Ave., Essex Junction, VT 05452 USA

Voice: 800-255-0562, 802-879-1164; Fax: 802-878-1768

Images for the PC and Macintosh. Subjects include logos and trademarks of leading companies, Accents & Attention Getters, Real Estate art, Safety & Packaging, Business Symbols, and others.

Jawai Interactive Inc.

Screen Caffeine Pro

501 East Fourth St. #511, Austin, TX 78701-3745 USA

Voice: 512-469-0502; Fax: 512-469-7850

Multimedia images for the Macintosh. Subjects include multimedia interface backgrounds, textures, and others.

Bruce Jones Design

Maps! Maps! Maps!

31 St. James Ave., Boston, MA 02116

Voice: 800-843-3873, 617-350-6160; Fax: 617-350-8764,

Internet: 76145.301@compuserve.com

Images for the PC and Macintosh. Subjects include World Maps, State-by-State, World Globes, and others.

Lanston Type Co. Ltd.

Clip Art Fonts

P.O. Box 60, Mount Stewart, Prince Edward Island, Canada C0A 1T0

Voice: 800-478-8973, 902-676-2835; Fax: 902-676-2393

Images and clip art fonts for the PC and Macintosh. Border and ornaments subjects include Fleurons, Granjon Folio, Folio One, Vine Leaves, and others.

Letraset USA

Fontek DesignFonts

40 Eisenhower Dr., Paramus, NJ 07653 USA

Voice: 800-343-8973, 201-845-6100; Fax: 201-845-5047

Featured in Chapter 15. See the Appendix for a special offer from Letraset USA. Clip art fonts and backgrounds for the PC and Macintosh. Subjects include Well Beings, Journeys, Industrials, Attitudes, Delectables, and others.

Library Educational Institute Inc. (LEI)

Library Clip Art

RR1 Box 219, New Albany, PA 18833 USA

Voice: 717-746-1842; Fax: 717-746-1114

Books and images for the PC and Macintosh. Library subjects include Children's Activities, Senior Citizens, Reading, Reference, Seasonal Events, and others.

17

Linographics Inc.

ScreenPrint Clip Art

770 N. Main St., Orange, CA 92668 USA

Voice: 800-854-0273, 714-639-0511; Fax: 714-639-3912

Images for the PC and Macintosh. Subjects include Mascots, Symbols, Tourist & Resort, Exotic Animals, People, and others.

Linotype-Hell Company

Clip Art Fonts

425 Oser Ave., Hauppauge, NY 11788 USA

Voice: 800-799-4922, 516-434-2000; Fax: 516-434-3616

Clip art fonts for the PC and Macintosh. Subjects include Caravan Borders, Auriol Flowers, Hot Metal Borders, Warning Pi, and others.

MacMedia Publications Inc.

MacAnatomy

5177 Richmond Ave. #1040, Houston, TX 77056 USA

Voice: 800-477-0717, 713-960-1858

Images for the PC and Macintosh. Medical subjects include an atlas of human anatomy and others.

Matsuri Graphics

JapanClips

P.O. Box 6926, Bloomington, IN 47407 USA

Voice: 812-336-1326; Fax: 812-339-5422

Internet: matsuri@intersource.com

Images for the PC and Macintosh. Traditional and modern Japanese subjects include Art & Religion, Gardens & Nature, Sports & Military, and others.

Medina Software Inc.

Clip Art Images

P.O. Box 521917, Longwood, FL 32752-1917 USA

Voice: 407-260-1676; Fax: 407-260-1636

Images for the Macintosh. Subjects include religion, electronics, and others.

metal Studio Inc.

Metal Graphic Image Collections

13164 Memorial Dr. #222, Houston, TX 77079 USA

Voice: 800-858-5254, 713-532-5177; Fax: 713-523-5176

Images for the PC and Macintosh. Subjects include symbols, icons, patterns, backgrounds, holidays, and others.

Metro Creative Graphics Inc.

Metro Subscription Service

33 West 34th St., New York, NY 10001 USA

Voice: 800-223-1600, 212-947-5100; Fax: 212-967-4602

Featured in Chapter 16. See the Appendix for a special offer from Metro Subscription Service. Subscription services for the PC and Macintosh. Subjects include Food & Fashion, Business & Borders, Seasonal Happenings, Holidays, and others.

MileStone Graphics

Golf, Beach, and Florida Clip Art Collections

1093 A1A Beach Blvd. #388, St. Augustine, FL 32084 USA

Voice: 800-932-5404, 904-823-9962; Fax: 904-824-6209,

Internet: 72142.1471@compuserve.com

Images for the PC and Macintosh. Subjects include symbolic, humorous, and realistic illustrations.

Monotype Typography Inc.

Clip Art Fonts

150 South Wacker Dr. #2630, Chicago, IL 60606 USA

Voice: 800-666-6897, 312-855-1440; Fax: 312-855-9475

Clip art fonts for the PC and Macintosh. Subjects include Arabesque, Contemporary Ornaments, Botanical Fun Font, Christmas Ornaments, Directions Pi Font, and others.

MOONLIGHTPRESS STUDIO

Stock art and custom illustration

362 Cromwell Ave., Ocean Breeze, NY 10305 USA

Voice: 718-979-9695; Fax: 718-979-8919

Stock illustrations sold on a per-image basis for the PC and Macintosh. Subjects include Buildings/Construction, Business, Home Accessories, People, Technology, and others.

Multi-Ad Services Inc.

ProArt

1720 W. Detweiller Dr., Peoria, IL 61615-1595 USA

Voice: 800-447-1950, 309-692-1530

Images for the PC and Macintosh. Subjects include Business, Sports, Holidays, People, and others.

Pretzel–from Metro Subscription Service. © 1995 Metro Creative Graphics. All rights reserved.

Pie–from the Florida Clip Art set. © 1995 MileStone Graphics. All rights reserved.

20

MvB Design

MvB Image Fonts
Available from FontHaus Inc.,
1375 Kings Highway East, Fairfield, CT 06430 USA
Voice: 800-942-9110, 203-367-1993; Fax: 203-367-1860
Featured in Chapter 17. See the Appendix for a special offer for MvB Design products. Clip art fonts for the PC and Macintosh. Subjects include FontHaus PictureFonts–Dick & Jane, AcmeGreenGarden, AcmeWhatever, Zoology 101, CatHaus, DogHaus, and others.

New Vision Technologies Inc.

Presentation Task Force and Publisher's Task Force
38 Auriga Dr. Unit 13, Nepean, Ontario, Canada K2E 8A5
Voice: 800-387-0732, 613-727-8184; Fax: 613-727-8190
Featured in Chapter 18. See the Appendix for a special offer from New Vision Technologies. Images for the PC and Macintosh. Subjects include Medical, Cartoons, Business, Industry, Technology, and others.

NIMX Foundry

Clip Art Fonts
3878 Oak Lawn Ave. #100B-177, Dallas, TX 75219-4610 USA
Voice: 800-688-6469; Fax: 214-350-8159
Clip art fonts for the PC and Macintosh. Subjects include Scat Dingbats, Jitterbats, Holiday Mix, Nature, and others.

Olduvai Corp.

ArtClips
9200 South Dadeland Blvd. #725, Miami, FL 33156 USA
Voice: 800-548-5151, 305-670-1112; Fax: 305-670-1992
Images and clip art fonts for the PC and Macintosh. Subjects include food, maps, sports, tools, office, and others.

One Mile Up Inc.

Federal Clip Art
7011 Evergreen Ct., Annandale, VA 22003 USA
Voice: 800-258-5280, 703-642-1177,
Fax: 703-642-9088
Images for the PC and Macintosh. Government subjects include A Congress of Art; Air, Naval, and Ground Combat; European Art; Insignia, and others.

The Oswego Company

Oswego Illustrated Archives

610 SW Alder St. #609, Portland, OR 97205 USA

Voice: 800-275-1989, 503-274-9338; Fax: 503-274-9326

Featured in Chapter 19. See the Appendix for a special offer from The Oswego Company. Images for the PC and Macintosh. Subjects include Architectural, Flora & Fauna, Home Electronics, Transportation & Travel, Business, and others.

Piano–from Oswego Illustrated Archives. © 1995 The Oswego Company. All rights reserved.

Pacific Rim Connections Inc.

Japanese & Chinese Clip Art

1838 El Camino Real #219, Burlingame, CA 94010 USA

Voice: 415-697-0911; Fax: 415-697-9439

Images for the PC and Macintosh. Subjects include calligraphy, yearly symbols, crests, patterns, scenes from Japanese culture, and others.

Page Studio Graphics

PIXymbols

3175 N. Price Rd. #1050, Chandler, AZ 85224 USA

Voice: 602-839-2763; Fax: 602-839-2763

Pictorial symbol fonts for the PC and Macintosh. Subjects include computer documentation, lodging & travel, hospital & safety, American Sign Language, phone buttons & symbols, and others.

21

Airliner–from Illustrated Stock Cuts. © 1995 Daniel Pelavin. All rights reserved.

Daniel Pelavin

Illustrated Stock Cuts

80 Varick St. #3B, New York, NY 10013 USA

Voice: 212-941-7418; Fax: 212-431-7138,

Internet: dpelavin@inch.com

Featured in Chapter 20. See the Appendix for a special offer from Daniel Pelavin. On-disk collection or stock illustrations sold on a per-image basis for the PC and Macintosh. Subjects include Food & Dining, Sports, Money & Finance, Health & Medicine, and others.

Hatbox–from the Past-Tints Sampler Edition. © 1995 Periwinkle Software. All rights reserved.

Periwinkle Software

Past-Tints

7475 Brydon Rd., La Verne, CA 91750 USA

Voice: 800-730-3556, 909-593-5062; Fax: 909-593-6062,

Internet: cs@periwinkle.com

Featured in Chapter 21. See the Appendix for a special offer from Periwinkle Software. Images for the PC and Macintosh. Subjects include Domestic Animals, People, Garden, Whimsy, and others.

Life preserver-from the CMCD Metaphorically Speaking set. © 1995 PhotoDisc Inc. All rights reserved.

PhotoDisc Inc.

CMCD Digital Photography
2013 Fourth Ave., Seattle, WA 98121 USA
Voice: 800-528-3472, 206-441-9355; Fax: 206-441-9379,
Internet: sales@photodisc.com(email)
Featured in Chapter 22. See the Appendix for a special offer from PhotoDisc. Images for the PC and Macintosh. Subjects include Metaphorically Speaking, Just Tools, Just Documents, Just Hands, Everyday Objects, and others.

Planet Art

Classic Graphics
505 S Beverly Dr., #242, Beverly Hills, CA 90212 USA
Voice: 818-878-9697; Fax: 818-878-9534
Images and photo clip art for the PC and Macintosh. Subjects include Textiles of India, Antique Maps, Icons, Arabic Tiles, Architecture, and others.

PolyType

PolyType Art Collection
P.O. Box 25976, Los Angeles, CA 90025 USA
Voice: 800-998-9934, 310-444-9934; Fax: 310-444-7897
Clip art fonts for the PC and Macintosh. Subjects include Business Icons, Optyx, Fruits & Vegetables, ArtDeco, Patterns, and others.

Reasonable Solutions Software

Art Solutions
1221 Disk Dr., Medford, OR 97501 USA
Voice: 800-876-3475, 503-776-5777; Fax: 503-773-7803
Images for the PC and Macintosh. Subjects include Education, Newsletters, Family Life, Tools, Travel, and others.

Richard Beatty Design

The Beatty Collection
2312 Laurel Park Hwy., Hendersonville, NC 28792 USA
Voice: 740-696-8316
Clip art fonts for the PC and Macintosh. Subjects include icons, symbols, ornaments, fleurons, needlework, and others.

Russell & Miller Inc. (R&M)

Clip art for retailers
12342 Bell Ranch Dr., Santa Fe Springs, CA 90670-3356 USA
Voice: 800-231-9600; Fax: 800-527-2488, 310-941-1654

22

Flower–from the Classic Graphics CD-ROM. © 1995 Planet Art. All rights reserved.

Images for the PC and Macintosh. Subjects include clothing, furniture, giftware, hardware, and others.

RT Computer Graphics Inc.

The Sante Fe Collection

602 San Juan De Rio, Rio Rancho, NM 87124 USA

Voice: 800-891-1600, 505-891-1600; Fax: 505-891-1350

Images for the PC and Macintosh. Native American subjects include sand paintings, weavings, symbols, pottery graphics, animals, and others.

Heart Tree–from the Valentines set. © 1995 SunShine. All rights reserved.

Software of the Month Club

Bright Ideas

5816 Dryden Pl., Carlsbad, CA 92008 USA

Voice: 800-433-0171, 619-931-8111; Fax: 619-931-8383

Subscription service for the PC and Macintosh. Subjects include business, industry, family, animals, travel, and others.

SunShine

Visual Delights

P.O. Box 4351, Austin, TX 78765 USA

Voice: 512-453-2334

Antique images for the PC and Macintosh. Subjects include Silhouettes, Children's Stories, Greek & Roman Life, Flower & Plant Cartouches, Reading & Writing, and others.

23

Judith Sutcliffe: The Electric Typographer

Clip Art Fonts

2216 Cliff Dr., Santa Barbara, CA 93109 USA

Voice: 805-966-7563

Clip art fonts for the PC and Macintosh. Subjects include Communications, Business & Services, Medical & Pharmaceutical, Military & Patriotic, Seals, and others.

Symbols–from the Petroglyph font. © 1995 Judith Sutcliffe: The Electric Typographer. All rights reserved.

T/Maker Company

ClickArt

1390 Villa St., Mountain View, CA 94041 USA

Voice: 800-9TMAKER (800-986-2537), 415-962-0195,

Fax: 415-962-0201, Internet: click_art@tmaker.com

Featured in Chapter 23. See the Appendix for a special offer from T/Maker. Images for the PC and Macintosh. Subjects include Artistry & Borders, Cartoons, Christian Illustrations, Occasions & Celebrations, Newsletter Art, and others.

Frog–from the ClickArt Studio Series. © 1995 T/Maker Company. All rights reserved.

TECH-M Company

Pop-In Parts and Pre-Drawn Standard Parts
9720 Executive Center Dr. #203, St. Petersburg, FL 33702 USA
Voice: 800-576-1881, 813-576-1884; Fax: 813-577-7207
Technical clip art for the PC and Macintosh. Subjects include
Network Symbols, Computer Parts, Schematic Symbols, Hands,
Circuit Card Components, and others.

TechPool Studios

LifeART Collections
1463 Warrensville Center Rd., Cleveland, OH 44121-2676 USA
Voice: 800-543-3278, 216-291-1922; Fax: 216-382-1915
Images for the PC and Macintosh. Subjects include Anatomy, Fire,
EMS, Emergency, Health Care, Dental, and others.

U-Design Type Foundry

Picture Fonts
270 Farmington Ave., Hartford, CT 06105 USA
Voice: 203-278-3648; Fax: 203-278-3003
Clip art fonts for the PC and Macintosh. Subjects include Symbols,
Ornaments, Tropical, Peculiars, DECOtations, and others.

24

Ultimate Symbol Inc.

Design Elements - A Digital Reference
31 Wilderness Dr., Stony Point, NY 10980 USA
Voice: 800-870-7940; Fax: 914-942-0004
Featured in Chapter 24. See the Appendix for a special offer from
Ultimate Symbol. Images for the PC and Macintosh. Subjects include
Stars/Suns/Moons/Zodiac, Flourishes/Accents/Typographical
Devices, Pictorial Symbols, Motifs/Shapes/Designs/Devices, Circular
Designs, Pointers/Arrows, Dingbats, and others.

Wayzata Technology Inc.

epsPRO
2515 East Hwy. 2, Grand Rapids, MN USA
Voice: 800-735-7321, 218-326-0597; Fax: 218-326-0598
Images for the PC and Macintosh. Subjects include Hollywood,
Medical, Cartoons, Shopping, Business, and others.

WEKA Publishing Inc.

Quality Clip Art Collection
1077 Bridgeport Ave., Shelton, CT 06484 USA
Voice: 800-222-9352; Fax: 203-944-3663

Images for the PC and Macintosh. Subjects include Art Elements, Business, Sports, Architecture, Leisure, and others.

Wheeler Arts

Quick Art
66 Lake Park, Champaign, IL 61821-7101 USA
Voice: 217-359-6816; Fax: 217-359-8716
Images for the PC and Macintosh. Subjects include Clothing & Sewing, Trees, Mail, Science & Energy, Weather, and others.

Whelan Design Studios

Whelan's ChurchArt
P.O. Box 51034, Denton, TX 76206 USA
Voice: 817-380-9514; Fax: 817-381-1913,
Internet: pvmv66a@prodigy.com
Images for the PC and Macintosh. Subjects include Events, Food, Ministries, Nursery & Family, Youth, and others.

Williams & Wilkins Electronic Media

Medical Illustration Library
351 W. Camden St., Baltimore, MD 21201-2436 USA
Voice: 800-527-5597, 410-528-4223; Fax: 410-528-4422
Images for the PC and Macintosh. Subjects include anatomically correct drawings by medical illustrator Diane Abeloff.

Youth Specialties Inc.

ArtSource
P.O. Box 4406, Spartanburg, SC 29305 USA
Voice: 800-776-8008, 803-573-7004; Fax: 803-583-7381,
Internet: youthspec@aol.com
Featured in Chapter 25. See the Appendix for a special offer from Youth Specialties. Images for the PC and Macintosh. Subjects include Fantastic Activities, Amazing Oddities & Appalling Images, Spiritual Topics, Attention Getters, Sports, and others.

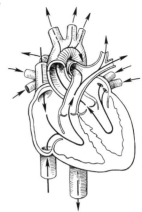

Heart–from the General Anatomy II Medical Illustration Library. © 1995 Williams & Wilkins. All rights reserved.

25

Camping–from ArtSource © 1995 Youth Specialties Inc. All rights reserved.

Chapter 2

Choose It

Choose It   You certainly wouldn't choose one book over another because it had more pages.

More of a good thing for your money, of course, makes sense. But with illustration—just as with books—quantity is no gauge of value.

If you doubt the value of high-quality illustrations, price a custom one. Even a simple black and white image by a proficient artist will typically cost at least $100. Color work by recognized illustrators begins in the thousands. In retrospect, good clip art is a bargain.

As any designer will tell you, the main criteria for choosing an image are a sound concept and a stylish execution. What it costs and what form it is in are only important if an illustration says what you want to say, the way that you want to say it.

28

Choosing a Concept

A good illustration is much more than mere ornamentation. At a minimum, it should grab attention and draw your reader into the message. At its best, it will express something words can't.

The clip art images that are the easiest to execute, and therefore the most common, are objects—something material such as a bouquet of flowers. By putting the bouquet in the context of a flier for a florist, you visually communicate the topic.

More interesting and less common are images that illustrate ideas or tell a story—such as the act of giving the flowers. These images are more interesting because they contribute meaning to your message, and they are less common because they are more difficult to conceive and are useful in fewer situations.

Once you begin to notice the subtleties of the visual language, you'll be better equipped to choose concepts that better illustrate your message. Some examples:

Bouquet–from the Family category of Megatoons Part II. © 1995 Creative Media Services. All rights reserved.

A CLICHÉ, for example, has a widely understood meaning. In this case, a skull and crossbones represents a danger to life.

Skull–from the Linotype Warning Pi font. © 1995 Linotype-Hell Company. All rights reserved.

An ICON is an image that suggests its meaning. The opened padlock represents the state of being unlocked.

Lock–from DigitArt, Universal Symbols. © 1995 Image Club Graphics Inc. All rights reserved.

A METAPHOR suggests a likeness between two ideas. Here, a half full/half empty glass of water is analogous to one's attitude about life.

Glass–from CMCD/ Metaphorically Speaking from PhotoDisc Inc. © 1995 CMCD Inc. All rights reserved.

29

A SIGN is a shorthand device that stands for something else. The @ sign, for example, represents *at.*

@–from the Minion font. © 1995 Adobe Systems Inc. All rights reserved.

A VISUAL PUN uses one or more symbols to create two or more possible meanings. In this illustration, the sharks' fins represent the concepts of money and caution.

Shark–from the Finance Set. © 1995 Art Parts. All rights reserved.

A SYMBOL is a visible image of something invisible. Here, an hourglass represents time.

Hourglass–from WetSet CD-ROM. © 1995 Dubl-Click Software Inc. All rights reserved.

Borders, rules, ornaments, and backgrounds typically are decorative elements used to break up space and enhance the overall design of the page.

As the audience for clip art grows, so too will the diversity and quality of the images and the ideas behind them.

Choosing a Style

If concept is what you say, style is how you phrase it. There are as many illustrative styles as there are illustrators. In fact, it is not uncommon for one artist to use several different styles.

These light bulbs give you some idea of that diversity.

While one artist simplifies the image to a series of basic shapes, another captures the contours and shading to achieve a completely different look and feel.

Style must be built on a strong foundation. It is said that to be a good abstract painter, you must first master realism. Although all good illustrators have not necessarily mastered realism, they understand basics such as the proportion of the human figure and the use of light, shade, and perspective. If you find it difficult to nail down whether inconsistencies in a drawing are part of an artist's style or simply poor execution, move on to another source.

And old is not necessarily bad. Like wide lapels and bell-bottom pants, illustrative styles come and go. It's not unusual to find artwork from past decades incorporated into the work of a world class design studio or advertising agency.

If you have space within your design to isolate one image from the next, you can often use more than one style. If the piece is small, or images are close, it's better to use a single style throughout.

The Clip Art Checklist

Beyond concept and style, judging a drawing is subjective—you either like it or you don't. But before you make your final selection, consider these issues.

INTEGRITY. Isolate the image from others around it. Twenty different images grouped together on the same page take on a personality of their own. To get a realistic view, cover the surrounding images and see if the artwork survives on its own.

31

Lightbulb 5–from the JCBingo font published by FontHaus. © 1995 Clinch Advertising. All rights reserved.

SIZE. View the image close to the size you will use it. Lots of images look terrific as tiny specks on a catalog page and not so terrific blown up to two or three inches across. Likewise, some images work better large than small.

SHAPE. Consider the shape of the overall image. A long horizontal image may not work well on a short vertical brochure cover. Organic shapes may require white space you simply can't spare.

32

Chapter 3

Use It

Use It It wasn't long ago that software and hardware technical issues limited the production and distribution of artwork on the computer.

The file formats used to store graphics information could not efficiently reproduce the detailed images artists created using conventional techniques. Editing and importing graphics required more computing horsepower than the average user could afford. Software programs that were capable of importing graphics often wouldn't import the file format you were working with. You could use clip art, but it was a challenge.

Today, those technical barriers have all but disappeared. There is a graphics file format for reproducing just about every technique imaginable. Though the size of a file can be large, the computing power of even entry-level machines is usually equal to the task. Virtually every desktop publishing, word processing, spreadsheet, and presentation software package has the tools to import, size, and crop clip art. Graphics software gives you the power to edit it. And just about any graphics, laser, or imagesetter will print it.

Once you understand which files work where, importing and printing clip art is a breeze.

The Ideal File Format

Most clip art images are stored as individual files. To use one, you open a word processing document, for example, and then import and place the image in position. When you print the document, the clip art file prints on the page which it was placed.

On the PC, clip art files are typically saved in one of a half-dozen or so formats—each stores the image information in a different way. It pays to know enough about these formats to choose the one that takes best advantage of your software and printer.

There are two basic ways to save graphic information. "Object-oriented" graphics, also referred to as draw or vector graphics, are created using geometric objects—lines, ovals, rectangles, and sometimes curves. The file stores information about the size, location, color, and so on, of each object.

The advantage of using object-oriented images is that you can use them as large or small as you like. The computer detects the change in size, recalculates the line weight, position, fill, and so on, and outputs the image using the highest resolution your printer can produce.

Clip art companies that produce object-oriented artwork typically use one or more of these formats: Adobe Illustrator (AI), Computer Graphics Metafile (CGM), Encapsulated PostScript (EPS), or Windows Metafile (WMF).

Bitmapped graphics, also referred to as paint or raster graphics, reproduce a more subtle, photographic-like image by dividing the artwork into a grid containing thousands of tiny dots or *pixels*. The size of a bitmapped file is often larger than an object-oriented file because it must store information about each of those pixels.

35

The size of the grid used to create the image establishes the resolution. An image created on a 200 pixel-per-inch (ppi) grid contains more detail than an image created on a 72 ppi grid. As you can imagine, drastically enlarging the image makes the grid pixels larger and more noticeable. Reducing the image forces the random elimination of pixels causing the artwork to deteriorate.

For that reason, object-oriented formats were, for a long time, the preferred formats. But advanced bitmapped formats such as the Tagged-Image File Format (TIFF) are better able to calculate and accommodate resizing. And though bitmapped files are often significantly larger than their object-oriented counterparts, mass storage CD-ROM and the increased speed and storage capacity of today's desktop computers make managing large files easier.

The result is that clip art companies are expanding their repertoire of illustration styles to take advantage of the extraordinary detail bitmapped formats can store. Some are using the increased latitude to offer images in two or more resolutions so that you can choose a version of the artwork that best suits your printer.

Clip art companies typically use these bitmapped formats: Kodak's ImagePak Photo CD format (PCD), PC Paintbrush (PCX), TIFF, or Windows Bitmap (BMP).

You can often identify an object-oriented image by its smooth fills and hard edged shapes. Shown here is a WMF image.

Father & son–from Publisher's Task Force. © 1995 New Vision Technologies. All rights reserved.

Soft edges and more natural tonal changes require a bitmapped file format. This is a TIFF image.

Father & daughter–from Electronic Clipper. © 1995 Dynamic Graphics Inc. All rights reserved.

37

Today, most clip art companies are producing images in formats that take the pros and cons of these formats into account. They obviously want their artwork to look as good as your system will allow. Clip art companies that cater to the broadest market keep their files small and distribute them in formats that don't require a PostScript printer. Companies that market primarily to professional desktop publishers assume that you have a PostScript printer with plenty of memory and a system that can use and process larger files.

Because all desktop publishing, word processing, and graphics software programs accept at least a few of the most common formats, you should choose the file format that matches the capabilities of the printer you will use to output the final page.

Using a Dot-Matrix Printer

While, in theory, the upper-end resolution of a dot-matrix printer (72 to 360 dots per inch (dpi)) matches that of a low-end laser printer, the inked ribbon technology doesn't produce the clarity, coverage, or tonal range necessary to reproduce anything but the most simple graphics.

If you're planning to print the final version of your project on a dot-matrix printer, use WMF object-oriented files when working with programs within Windows and use CGM files when working with programs that run under DOS. You can compose and preview documents using PostScript EPS files on your non-PostScript printer (you get a printout of the crude representation that appears on your computer screen), but you'll have to print the final file on a PostScript printer or imagesetter to get high-resolution results. TIFF and PCX are the logical bitmapped choices.

Using an Inkjet or Non-PostScript Laser Printer

If your final artwork will be output on an inkjet or non-PostScript laser printer, use WMF object-oriented files when you're working with programs within Windows and use CGM files when working with programs that run under DOS. You can compose and preview documents using PostScript EPS files on your non-PostScript printer (you get a printout of the crude representation that appears on your computer screen), but you'll have to print the final file on a PostScript printer or imagesetter to get high-resolution results.

38

You should be able to print any of the bitmapped formats your software program allows you to place. The only obvious limiting factor is the amount of memory your printer has to process the image. If you cannot print a large or complex image, insufficient printer memory is often the culprit.

Using a PostScript Laser Printer

A PostScript laser printer is able to reproduce a wider range of graphic effects than its non-PostScript counterparts can reproduce. As a result, PostScript has become the de facto standard for high-end desktop publishing. Manufacturers that include the PostScript interpreter within their printers pay a fee to Adobe Systems, PostScript's developer. Hence, PostScript printers are often a bit more expensive.

PostScript clip art is created using a PostScript drawing program that allows the artist to create graceful curves and fill shapes with more complex patterns and colors. These advantages are considered so important that some clip art companies produce their images in PostScript form only.

If you have a PostScript printer, choose PostScript files (usually EPS) over WMF or CGM files, especially when you are using images that include fluid shapes and/or gradient fills.

As with non-Postscript printers, you should be able to print any of the bitmapped formats your software program allows you to place. The only obvious limiting factor is the amount of memory your printer has to process the image. If you cannot print a large or complex image, insufficient printer memory is often the culprit.

39

Printer–from Publisher's Task Force. © 1995 New Vision Technologies. All rights reserved.

Using a PostScript Imagesetter

An imagesetter is a supercharged version of a PostScript laser printer. Whereas an ordinary laser printer produces 300 dpi or 600 dpi on plain paper, an imagesetter prints at 1,200 dpi, 2,400 dpi, or higher on photographic paper or film. The resulting output is typically used to create plates for a commercial printing press.

If you don't want to shell out tens of thousands of dollars to buy your own imagesetter, you can buy output by the page through a commercial printer or service bureau that specializes in offering high-resolution printouts. Check your Yellow Pages under Computer Graphics, Desktop Publishing, Printers, or Typesetting.

The same file formats recommended for the PostScript laser printer on the preceding page apply to the imagesetter.

Other Output Options

A printer is not the only kind of output device. Presentation software and multimedia authoring programs provide the tools to import and manipulate graphics.

You can create a series of screen pages, output on a film recorder to 35mm slides, and project them 20 feet across on an auditorium stage. Or you can output images to a computer screen as part of an animated business presentation.

Using Clip Art in Font Form

Much of today's most interesting art is a mere keystroke away. Companies that have traditionally focused on the design and distribution of fonts are now offering clip art in font form. Some clip art fonts are made up of simple icons or symbols, others provide the pieces for creating borders and frames, and still others contain spot illustrations every bit as complete as their full-size counterparts.

Rather than importing a separate file, you type the character that corresponds with the image you've chosen and reduce or enlarge it by changing the font size.

The format issues are simple in comparison to graphics file formats. There are two mainstream font formats on the PC—PostScript and TrueType. Most clip art fonts are offered in either format. As with conventional images, if your final document will be printed on a PostScript device, choose the PostScript version. If you plan to print to a non-PostScript printer only, the TrueType font format is adequate.

TrueType users who find a PostScript font that does not have a TrueType version can use Adobe Type Manager (ATM) to print PostScript fonts to a non-PostScript printer.

The Clip Art Toolbox

Once you understand the rules, you learn to break them. Electronic clip art has a major advantage over its cut-and-paste cousin. You can convert it to other formats and port it to other platforms. You can manage it with ease and speed. And you can transform it with all manner of high-tech tools.

Use Any Image Anywhere

Paperwork–from the Son of Business set. © 1995 Art Parts. All rights reserved.

The file formats discussed to this point are those most frequently used by commercial clip art producers, but they are by no means the only formats.

Suppose you have a WordPerfect Graphics (WPG) object-oriented file that your program won't recognize. Or a PostScript EPS image and no PostScript printer. Maybe you've got a bitmapped image that you want to change to object-oriented, or vice versa. The answer to these and other graphics incompatibilities is a graphics conversion program.

Two examples:

Transverter Pro translates any PostScript EPS or AI clip art file into an editable PostScript file or a non-PostScript object-oriented or bitmapped file. It also allows you to automate time-consuming tasks such as converting color images to grayscale, and grayscale to line. From Techpool Software Inc., 1463 Warrensville Ctr. Rd., Cleveland, OH 44121-2676 USA, Voice: 800-925-6998, 216-291-1922; Fax: 216-382-1915

At last count HiJaak Pro converts images between more than 50 object-oriented and bitmapped file formats—no small feat when you consider all the variables. You can get from just about any clip art image to mainstream formats such as CorelDraw's CDR and AutoCAD's DXF. The conversion tools allow you to control everything from color to the number of line segments used to define a curve. Inset Systems Inc., 71 Commerce Dr., Brookfield, CT 06804 USA, Voice: 800-374-6738, 203-740-2400; Fax: 203-775-5634

Organize Your Images

Your clip art toolbox will also likely include a program for organizing and searching for images—a "browser" to supplement your standard hardcopy catalog of printouts. You'll get some hands-on experience with this as you begin to use the *Clip Art Crazy CD-ROM*. The Kudo Catalog Reader included on the CD-ROM allows you to search for images by subject, file size, filename, and so on, to see a thumbnail view of the actual image, and to drag and place artwork in your software programs. The commercial version includes the tools you need to create catalogs of your own clip art and photographs. Imspace Systems Corp., 2665 Ariane Dr. #207, San Diego, CA 92117-3422 USA, Voice: 800-488-5836, 619-272-2600; Fax: 619-272-4292, Internet: http://www.imspace.com.

Editing Clip Art

Both the boon and the bane of using clip art is the fact that you can edit it—a boon, because a skilled artist can change an image or use it as the seed of a new idea; a bane because it doesn't always work.

To edit an image you need a tool similar to the one used to create it. Object-oriented images are most often born from sophisticated drawing programs such as Adobe Illustrator and CorelDraw. If you already have such a program, look no further. It provides all the tools you need to edit AI, most EPS, CGM, and WMF clip art files and it allows you to export the files to other file formats.

Bitmapped clip art is typically scanned and then cleaned up in a paint program. The current crop of full-featured paint programs run circles around their predecessors. Graphics hybrids such as Adobe Photoshop and Fractal Design Painter allow you to create everything from simple laser-quality artwork to the kind of high-resolution photographic illustrations you see on the pages of national magazines. If you've got the system to run them and the patience to learn, you can work real magic.

Another, less expensive alternative, is the HiJaak Graphics Suite. In addition to the HiJaak conversion program, mentioned on the opposite page, the graphics suite includes HiJaak Draw for editing object-oriented images, HiJaak TouchUp for editing bitmapped graphics, and a browser. Inset Systems Inc., 71 Commerce Dr., Brookfield, CT 06804 USA, Voice: 800-374-6738, 203-740-2400; Fax: 203-775-5634

43

Some clip art companies even include simple graphics tools and browsers as part of their product. New Vision Technologies, for example, includes Task Force Commander For Windows with its PC clip art collections. Commander lets you change colors, convert color to grayscale or black and white, and create backdrops.

If you plan to edit object-oriented art, the way the artist arranged the objects within the file can make your job easier. Many of the companies "layer" their images so that individual elements can be removed or repositioned.

The editing possibilities are unlimited. Using the appropriate drawing or paint program you can select an image . . .

Flop or rotate it . . .

Add grayscales or colors . . .

Add a shadow . . .

Change the angle . . .

45

Use special effects . . .

Add type, other images, and more . . .

The Legal Side of Clip Art

For safety's sake, it is best to assume that all visual material is copyrighted until you find out otherwise. Beginning in 1978 a work was automatically protected from the moment of its creation and is ordinarily given a copyright term of the author's life, plus 50 years. Though the law prior to 1978 was not as comprehensive, it's a safe bet that lots of pre-1978 material is also protected for many years to come. Although the familiar copyright symbol (©) is often used to alert users that a particular image or publication is copyrighted, even that notice is not always necessary.

Justice–from Electronic Clipper. © 1995 Dynamic Graphics Inc. All rights reserved.

And just because you change an image doesn't nullify the existing copyright and confer it to you.

In the *Legal Guide for the Visual Artist* (Allworth Press, New York, 1995), Tad Crawford writes "What is the test for copyright infringement? It is whether an ordinary observer, looking at the original work and the work allegedly copied from it, recognizes that a copying has taken place." You'll have to make some serious changes to pass that test.

46

With the advent of hardware and software tools that make copying tantalizingly simple, the illustration and photography communities are taking legal action against folks who refuse to play by the rules. If you see an image you must have, the common sense approach is to contact the publisher for permission.

License and Use Agreements

Before you use clip art from any source you should read the legalese. Although many license and use agreements are similar, there are important differences. For example, while virtually all clip art companies allow you to use their images in a brochure or newsletter, some will not allow you to use the images on a T-shirt, poster, or other projects where the image constitutes a substantial portion of the value of what you are creating.

All include a clause that says you can't republish an image, or any part of an image, for anything that even remotely smacks of clip art.

47

Companies that sell individual "stock" illustrations typically hold an even tighter rein on their creations by selling the rights to reproduce an image for a specific project or use. Those charges may be based on the kind of project you are creating, the size of the audience, a combination of the two, or other criteria. Suffice it to say that when you are using someone else's art, reading and understanding these agreements is critical.

The reason you and I have access to such a superb selection of artwork is because some very talented people are able to make a living conceiving it, creating it, and selling it. You can protect their livelihood by urging others not to reproduce copyrighted material and not to distribute or accept files they did not pay for.

Using Artwork From *Clip Art Crazy*

There are 25 images from each of 20 different companies included on the *Clip Art Crazy CD-ROM* and cataloged beginning on page 159. These companies have contributed samples in the hope that you will use them, like them, and order more.

As with any copyrighted clip art, when you purchased this book, you bought the right to use the artwork; you don't own it. There are text files from each company located on the *Clip Art Crazy CD-ROM*. Each manufacturer has included license information in that file. Please read and heed this important information before you use the images provided by each of the companies.

Images used to illustrate this book that are not included on the CD-ROM are for your eyes only. They, too, are copyrighted material—please do not reproduce any image. Instead, note the name of the company in the caption, find the company's listing in Chapter 1, and buy the artwork directly from them.

Cartoon by Sidney Harris–from Famous Magazine Cartoons published by T/Maker. © 1995 Sandhill Arts. All rights reserved.

"Of course they always tell you to make changes—that's because you always tell them how <u>easy</u> it is to make changes."

Part II

Clip Art Projects

51

Clip Art Projects The ancient Chinese proverb says "One picture is worth more than ten thousand words."

In the nineteenth century the novelist Tregeneb wrote "A picture shows me at a glance what it takes dozens of pages of a book to expound." Today, in the dawn of the twenty-first century, rocker Rod Stewart sings "Every picture tells a story don't it." So much for Darwin's theory.

The true measure of stock illustrations and clip art is how readily you can apply them to real, practical projects. Chapters 4 and 5 present 50 out-of-the-ordinary projects designed to demonstrate the power of pictures.

All of the projects were created specifically for *Clip Art Crazy*, so when you see something you like, you can copy the design, clip art, typeface choices, and even the headline and text ideas, without stepping on toes.

52

Chapter 4 • Business Projects focuses on using clip art to improve your business communications. Not as mere decoration, but to grab attention, build your image, and sell your products and services.

Chapter 5 • Just for Fun explores some of the crazier stuff—how to use images that you love but can't find a practical use for, and ways to use clip art purely for art's sake.

How the projects are organized

Each project includes a general description, an explanation of the example, pointers for creating your own version, a list of image credits, and sources for related products and services.

But the photograph holds most of the information. Each project includes one or more views of the finished piece laid out so you can see how it was assembled, printed, folded,

trimmed, and/or bound. In the box on the right side of the photograph you'll find a tidbit about the project pictured or clip art in general.

You might think of them as "idea maps," part of an atlas that begins to show you the many different directions you can travel applying stock illustrations and clip art to real world designs.

Bon voyage.

Guitar–from the People category of Publisher's Task Force Volume 1. Chimpanzee (no offense Rod)–from the Animals category of Presentation Task Force. © 1995 New Vision Technologies. All rights reserved.

53

Building–from Assorted Images Volume 1. © 1995 Harter Image Archives. All rights reserved.

Lightbulb on the fourth floor–from Dick & Jane by Mark van Bronkhorst (product in font format). © 1995 MvB Design. All rights reserved.

Chapter 4

Business Projects

Advertisement Before your ad can romance customers into a sale, it's got to keep them from turning the page.

A simple device like this illustrated headline attempts to slow them down long enough to get them interested—in this case by challenging them to guess the missing words.

The example uses a rectangular format to offer a prospectus for an investment company via an 800 number. But it's easy to see how your version could employ a longer headline and more images to fill just about any ad space.

The illustrations can be simple like these or significantly more complex. The key ingredient is that the headline typeface be unobtrusive enough that the pictures don't fight the words.

56

Opposite: Car, pig, house, lightbulb—from Dick & Jane by Mark van Bronkhorst (product in font format). © 1995 MvB Design. All rights reserved.

You can spend your savings on a fancy new , risk it on  belly futures, sink it into a little  at the lake or invest it in a bright

The Sampler Group invests in sound companies with bright ideas. Place your text in this position. To achieve the same look, choose a similar font and duplicate the size, spacing, and alignment. For a free prospectus, call 800-987-6543.

Serious uses for funny stuff. Think twice before you discount humorous clip art as frivolous. Used judiciously, humor can deliver a message people will remember.

57

Basic Brochure Your organization's brochure is the run-of-the-mill stuff that keeps the mill running.

It's an inexpensive, flexible format for telling your story; for selling your product, service, or company capabilities; and for supplying the impetus and information for taking action.

When you don't have the time or budget to use illustrations of your product or service in action, a well-chosen stock illustration creates a focal point from which to build.

This example uses a single image to set the mood. Both the headline and the illustration evolve as you unfold the panels. The rose is printed in a light tone on the cover (top), in a slightly darker tone on the second panel (middle), and in its full glory on the third (bottom).

The brochure is printed on a standard 11-by-8 $\frac{1}{2}$-inch sheet and folded to fit a #10 business envelope.

58

Opposite: Rose–from Assorted Images Volume 1. © 1995 Harter Image Archives. All rights reserved.

The mix of artwork and typefaces is key to establishing a mood. If you're not ready to create your own combinations, try those used here and on the pages that follow.

59

Bulletin A bulletin is a step short of a newsletter.

It provides news and information in a streamlined format—
fast and easy to update and edit.

In this example, *ON BELAY*, a term used by climbers, is
used as the masthead, and climber's tools are used as the
illustration. The month of issue and the name of the organization are listed in the left-hand column. You can use the same
illustration for each issue or you can change it a little each
time.

The bulletin is printed on a standard 8 ½-by-14-inch sheet.
You can use one or both sides, fold it as shown at the right, and
mail it in a #10 business envelope, or you can adapt the design
to a self-mailer.

60

*Opposite: Carabiners, ice
axe–from Tom Parker's
Icontents-Volume 32.
© 1995 Image Club
Graphics Inc. All rights
reserved.*

See how the tone background shows through the negative areas of the clip art image? It's one of the simple technical enhancements to look for in a good clip art collection.

61

Business Book If you have more information than a conventional brochure will hold, try creating a version of this business book.

This layout and saddle-stitched binding (bound with staples) accommodates as few as 8 pages and as many as 32 or more. Each 11-by-8 $^1/_2$-inch sheet holds 4 book pages—2 on each side. Your book can contain any combination of 4 pages.

The example shows how a symphony orchestra might promote a season of music programs—one page for each night. There's space for an introduction in the front and for contact information and an order form in the back.

62

Opposite: Piano–from the Musical Instruments category of the Oswego Illustrated Archives. © 1995 Oswego Company. All rights reserved.

Drum set–from the Music category of Publisher's Task Force Volume 1. © 1995 New Vision Technologies Inc. All rights reserved.

Flute–from Worldbeat America-Volume 31. © 1995 Image Club Graphics Inc. All rights reserved.

This is a good example of how you can mix different clip art styles within a single design. The images emphasize the musical themes for each night.

63

Business Card Does your business card do some selling?

Does it clearly state your stock and trade? Does it reflect your style? If not, try a layout that does all three.

The tease half of the headline is positioned above the cut and the cover image; the payoff falls below the image inside. Your version might include these basics plus a mission statement, your title, e-mail and/or Internet address, home phone, hours of operation, post office box number—any of a number of pieces of information that match your needs.

The color background on the cover can be printed with ink, or you can ask your local commercial printer to reproduce the card on duplex stock—two sheets of paper glued together and available in a variety of color combinations.

64

Opposite: Ship, Tower Bridge–from the Journeys Fontek DesignFont. © 1995 Letraset USA. All rights reserved.

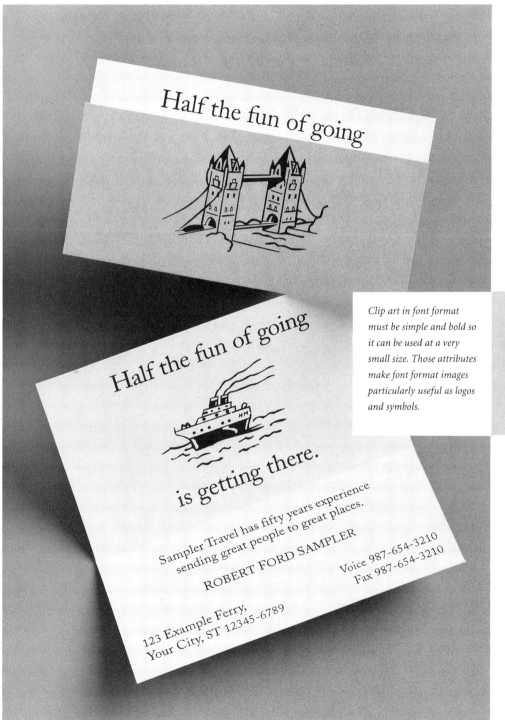

Clip art in font format must be simple and bold so it can be used at a very small size. Those attributes make font format images particularly useful as logos and symbols.

Button Whether you use it as a badge, a souvenir, a walking billboard, or an ID, a button is an inexpensive, do-it-yourself project perfectly suited for the desktop.

The "Magic Night" example promotes an event, in this case a fund raiser; the automobile button is used to identify a rallye official; and the "Hot Shot" button serves as a prize for "broker of the month."

The process is simple—you print your artwork on plain paper, trim it out using a circle cutter, sandwich the cutout between the metal and plastic button parts, and seal the finished button with a special press.

Need do-it-yourself button machines and parts? These examples were mounted on a button machine from U.S.A. Buttons Inc., 175 Progress Dr., West Bend, WI 53095 USA Voice: 800-777-4992, 414-334-4748; Fax: 414-334-1220.

66

Opposite: Top hat with magic wand–from the A*I Eclectic font. © 1995 Alphabets Inc. All rights reserved.

Bull–from MacGallery II. © 1995 Dream Maker Software. All rights reserved.

Car–from the FontHaus PictureFonts Transportation & Travel (product in font format). © 1995 MvB Design. All rights reserved.

Before you lay out any project, first consider the distance from which it will be viewed.

Calendar With so many business people organizing their schedules using off-the-shelf calendars, it's easy to see how an industry-specific calendar poses a valuable marketing opportunity.

The example demonstrates how a radio station might use a calendar to help clients plan their advertising. This generic layout squeezes an entire month onto a single page. The user enters the name of the month on the top line and uses as many lines as necessary—one for each day. The column to the left allows space for essential marketing and contact information.

A commercial printer can print the calendars in quantity and assemble them as pads.

68

Opposite: Microphone–
from the Cartoon 1
category of Publisher's Task
Force Volume 1. © 1995
New Vision Technologies
Inc. All rights reserved.

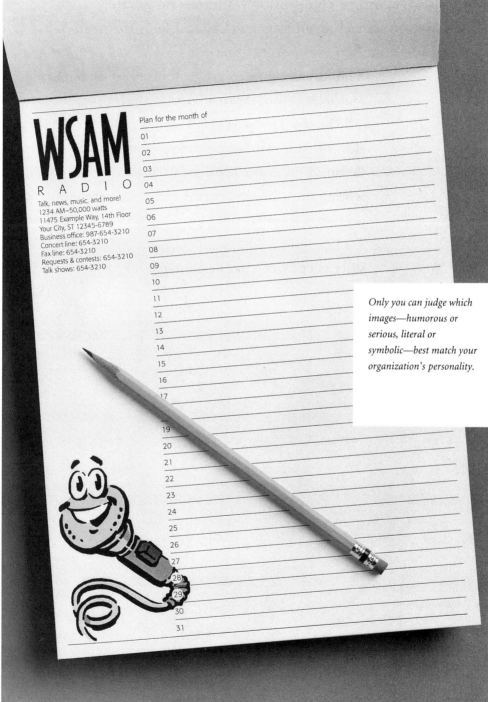

Plan for the month of
01
02
03
04
05
06
07
08
09
10
11
12
13
14
15
16
17
19
20
21
22
23
24
25
26
27
28
29
30
31

WSAM
R A D I O
Talk, news, music, and more!
1234 AM–50,000 watts
11475 Example Way, 14th Floor
Your City, ST 12345-6789
Business office: 987-654-3210
Concert line: 654-3210
Fax line: 654-3210
Requests & contests: 654-3210
Talk shows: 654-3210

Only you can judge which images—humorous or serious, literal or symbolic—best match your organization's personality.

69

Certificate Simple recognition—there is no greater compensation for achievement, service, and dedication than a simple "well done."

A fitting image gives an award a distinctive look and feel, something beyond the typical cookie-cutter designs.

The example names a "Firefighter of the Year." The basic elements include the name of the presenter and the recipient, the title of the award, a paragraph that describes why the award is being given, the date, and the names and signatures of the organization's principals.

Print your finished certificate on a standard 11-by-8 $\frac{1}{2}$-inch sheet and present it in a simple frame.

70

Opposite: Fire truck–from the Transit category of Publisher's Task Force Volume 1. © 1995 New Vision Technologies Inc. All rights reserved.

An illustration like this accomplishes something words cannot—instant atmosphere, a visual environment for your words to operate in.

Chart Charts and graphs don't have to be boring *or* complicated.

The example provides a simple model for using an illustration to transmit the subject of your data. The trick is to use an image with a minimum of distinct darks and lights—something that won't overpower the information.

Each horizontal bar represents the percentage of one dollar spent on a fictional food budget. The scale on the left tallies the total.

The chart is mounted in a standard sheet protector and displayed in a Pro-Show Binder that converts to a display easel. Both are from 20th Century Plastics, 205 South Puente St., Brea, CA 92621 USA, Voice: 800-767-0777, 714-441-4500; Fax: 714-441-4550.

72

Opposite: Food–from ArtSource Volume One-Fantastic Activities. © 1995 Youth Specialties Inc. All rights reserved.

At times what makes an image relevant to a design is the mere fact that it evokes a feeling or establishes a look or quality.

73

Counter Card A lack of information can be a missed opportunity. A counter card offers instructions, sells a product or service, or supplies information—24 hours a day.

The example shows how a sporting goods store might publicize fishing and hunting licenses. Although such details might not merit permanent signs or significant attention, a counter card is an inexpensive way to answer often-asked questions, to test offers before you advertise them, or to present policies.

There are all manner of holders and easels to display various size cards. This example is displayed in a crystal-clear acrylic holder from the retail merchandising products catalog of Russell & Miller Inc., 12342 Bell Ranch Dr., Santa Fe Springs, CA 90670-3356 USA, Voice: 800-231-9600; Fax: 800-527-2488, 310-941-1654.

Opposite: Deer–from the Adobe Carta font. © 1995 Adobe Systems Inc. All rights reserved.

Fish–from the Past-Tints Sampler Edition. © 1995 Periwinkle Software. All rights reserved.

Try using an image within an image. The deer icon provides a good visual contrast to the complex fish illustration.

75

Coupon When your offer is one of 50 in a mailing, it had better have some stopping power.

A compelling offer and an unusual image is the kind of combination that wins prospects. The coupon example has space for two clip art images, a bold offer headline, some explanatory text, your company name, and a big phone number.

76

If you find a clip art collection that perfectly matches your needs, consider using it as the exclusive source of images for all your ads, brochures, newsletters, and so on.

Direct Mailer You might call this a "boomerang mailer"—a single piece that you mail out and the customer returns.

How? The panel with the piggy bank image (top) is used to address and mail the offer. The prospect reads the headline, in this case "A great vacation begins with a dream." and opens it for the payoff: "And a plan."

The "Tell us your dream" panel and the panel just above it separate from the rest of the mailer to create a sealed, postpaid business reply envelope for returning a check and a secure area for writing credit card information.

Need a custom-printed mailer? The example was designed using a standard format (Model F) from Champion Printing Inc., 3250 Spring Grove Ave., Cincinnati, OH 45225 USA, Voice: 800-543-1957, 513-541-1100; Fax: 513-541-9398.

78

Opposite: Dance, guitar, piggy bank, sunbathing, swimming, waiter–from Designer's Club Service. © 1995 Dynamic Graphics Inc. All rights reserved.

Note how the single, multifaceted image from the cover is divided and its parts are used to illustrate the inside.

Fax Cover Sheet As worldwide communications minimize the importance of place, you can trumpet local pride by showing people where you're from.

These examples show how you might use a local landmark or a distinctive skyline to emphasize the fact that you're in a nearby town or a city halfway around the world.

Compose your version on half of an 8 $1/2$-by-11-inch sheet to conserve paper and be sure to include, at a minimum, to whom the message is addressed, the name of the organization, your name and phone number, the date and time, a number for inquiring about transmission problems, and the number of pages to follow.

80

Opposite: Seattle, Washington skyline–from the Electronic Clipper Service. © 1995 Dynamic Graphics Inc. All rights reserved.

Big Ben clock tower, London, England–from the Electronic Clipper Service. © 1995 Dynamic Graphics Inc. All rights reserved.

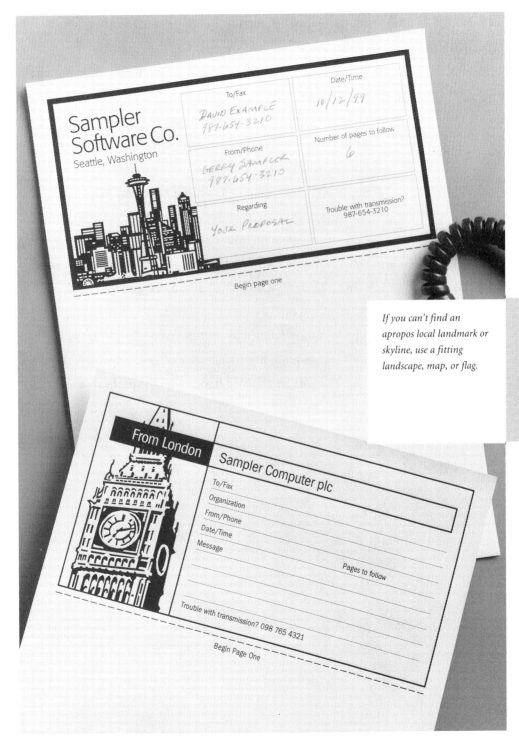

If you can't find an apropos local landmark or skyline, use a fitting landscape, map, or flag.

81

Greeting Card Solemn or silly, clip art is a perfect venue for greeting cards.

In its simplest form, the cover image sets the stage for the text inside.

The example shows an invitation but the format works equally as well for business or personal holiday greetings, birthdays, anniversaries, thank you's, congratulations, or for announcing events such as a name change or a move. An invitation typically includes the name of the host or organization, the day, date, and hour, the location, phone number, and, if necessary, an R.S.V.P—*respondez si'l vous plaît,* "please reply."

The photograph includes both folded and unfolded versions of the card. For it to read correctly, use the graphics and text rotation feature of your desktop publishing or word processing program to turn one panel upside down. A standard 8 $\frac{1}{2}$-by-11-inch sheet folded in quarters fits perfectly in an A2-style envelope.

82

Opposite: Grapes–from Metro Subscription Service. © 1995 Metro Creative Graphics Inc. All rights reserved.

Add interest to a black-and-white project by using contrasting paper colors or textures. This invitation is printed on dark paper and mailed in a light-colored envelope.

Discover
Sampler Island
WINES

Join us on Thursday, February 12th
for the first area tasting of wines from three
small vineyards on the northern coast of
Sampler Island.

6:30 P.M. to 8:00 P.M.
Example Inn, 123 Sampler Lock, Your City
Sponsored by Example Distributors
987-654-3210

R.S.V.P.

Illustrated Envelope Like it or not, you've got no more than a split second to convince a customer to open your envelope.

No matter how compelling the information inside, for that moment, the envelope makes or breaks the entire mailing.

These examples show how three different types of businesses—a travel agency, a janitorial service, and a real estate agency—might create interest using the same basic design with different headlines and artwork.

For small mailings you can have a commercial printer reproduce your artwork on ready-made envelopes, but for mass mailings you will likely get better results and a lower price by having your image printed on paper before the envelope is assembled.

84

Opposite: Airliner, house, listen–from Illustrated Stock Cuts. © 1995 Daniel Pelavin. All rights reserved.

When you have a series of oddly shaped images that must each fit roughly into the same area, use an identical shape such as an oval or a box to make them visually equivalent.

85

Instant Flier Just because a flier is fast and inexpensive doesn't mean it should be any less elegant than a corporate brochure.

The example demonstrates how a cleaning service might prospect for new customers. All of the essential elements are included—the company name and contact information, a list of services, a detailed description, and a call to action with a bold phone number.

The two variations show how something as simple as adjusting the tone of the images can dramatically change the look of the finished piece.

86

Opposite: Butterfly, flowers–from Assorted Images Volume 1. © 1995 Harter Image Archives. All rights reserved.

Although your first instinct may be to choose images that literally illustrate your subject, in some cases, a larger concept or theme produces more interesting results.

87

Letterhead Any document that is as widely circulated as your
letterhead deserves some serious thought.

And more often than not, the principal element is your logo.

A logo is a tangible representation of your organization's
character, visual device that is uniquely yours. It's not unusual
for a large corporation to spend tens of thousands of dollars in
developing one. Although it is risky to adopt a well circulated
clip art image as your logo (someone else might use it as well),
it is far less of a gamble to use a combination of two or more
images.

Opposite: Snowflake, sun, wheat–from Design Elements–A Digital Reference. © 1995 Ultimate Symbol Inc. All rights reserved.

Each of the examples shown here uses a combination of two
clip art images to represent a unique concept—a sun symbol
and a snowflake represent hot and cold, a heart and a wheat
stalk illustrate a food bank, and a paint roller and type ornament that appear to produce wallpaper represent a decorator.

88

Heart–from Altemus Borders Three. © 1995 Altemus Creative Services. All rights reserved.

Paint roller–from Universal Symbols-Volume 17. © 1995 Image Club Graphics Inc. All rights reserved.

Wallpaper ornament–from the Adobe Caslon Ornaments font. © 1995 Adobe Systems Inc. All rights reserved.

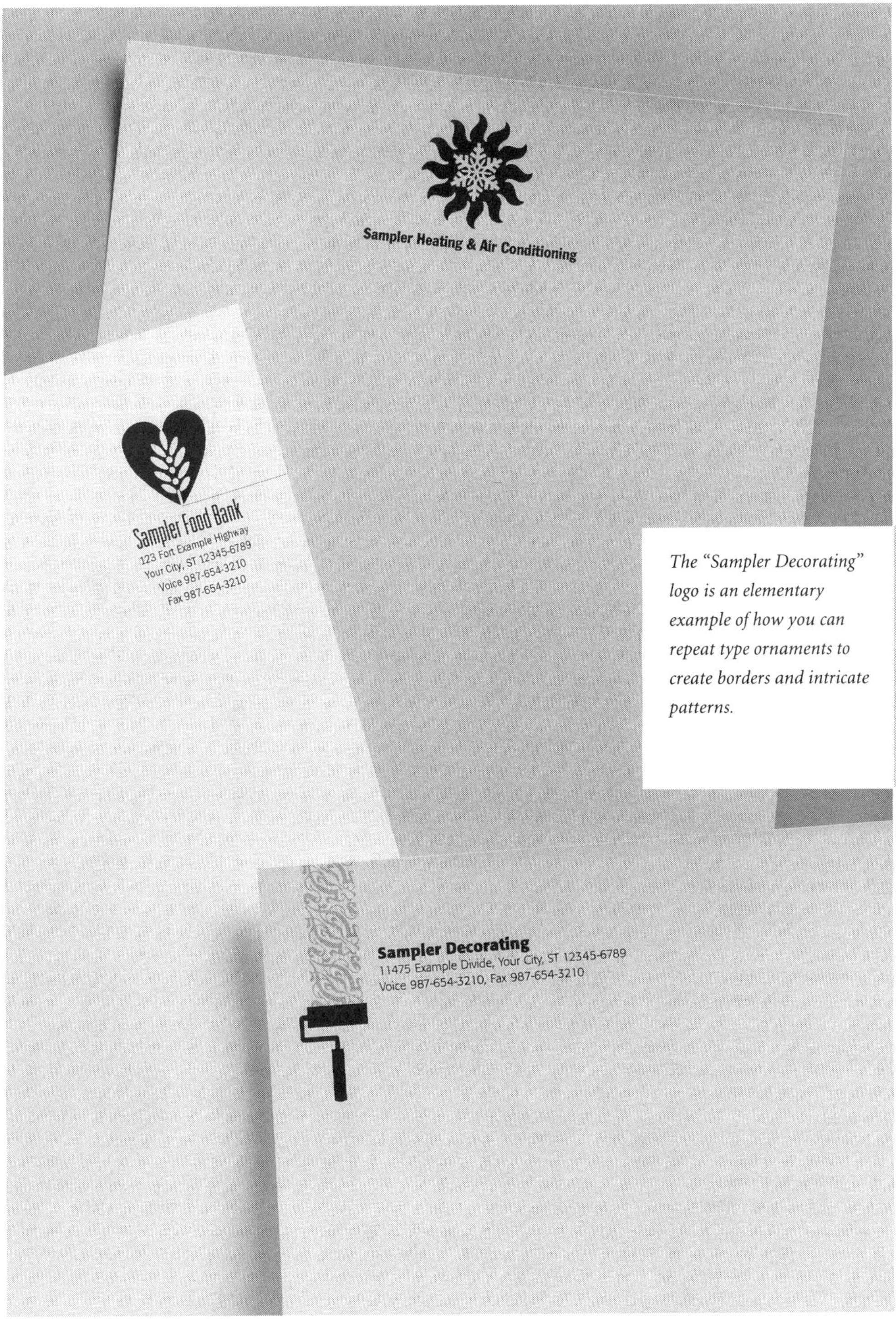

Sampler Heating & Air Conditioning

Sampler Food Bank
123 Fort Example Highway
Your City, ST 12345-6789
Voice 987-654-3210
Fax 987-654-3210

The "Sampler Decorating" logo is an elementary example of how you can repeat type ornaments to create borders and intricate patterns.

89

Sampler Decorating
11475 Example Divide, Your City, ST 12345-6789
Voice 987-654-3210, Fax 987-654-3210

Map Words and pictures tell a story with an ease that words alone cannot.

The example maps out the admission, parking, concession, and staging areas for a festival. Roads and designated areas are plotted using simple boxes and lines.

Your version could include a larger view that provides directions to your place of business, to an event, or leads prospects to a property for sale.

Opposite: Bus, car, dollar sign, first aid cross, knife and fork, man, seated figure, telephone, woman/ man–from Universal Symbols-Volume 17. © 1995 Image Club Graphics Inc. All rights reserved.

Arrow, sound speaker–from Objects & Icons-Volume 26. © 1995 Image Club Graphics Inc. All rights reserved.

You can easily change the focus of an image by tacking on a word or phrase. The seated figure, for example—a waiting area icon—is used here to represent audience seating.

91

Menu In the restaurant business, ambience is second only to food. And a good part of the mood is established with the presentation of a menu. In this case, with such a powerful image, a minimum of text and a modest design allow the image to work its magic—less is more.

This menu is in booklet form. The finished piece is 8 inches square and saddle stitched (bound with staples). A detail from the cover is repeated on the edge of each inside page.

A menu is your chance to use images that amplify the atmosphere and communicate the personality of the people behind the scenes.

Opposite: Still life painting by Van Kessel–from the Dutch Masters Volume. © 1995 Planet Art. All rights reserved.

SAMPLER CAFE

Desserts

PRODUCT NAME. Place your text in this position. To achieve the same look, choose a similar font and duplicate the size, spacing. $1.00

PRODUCT NAME. To match the overall page design, choose a clip art image of roughly the same weight and density, and duplicate its positioning and proportion to the other elements on the page. $2.00

PRODUCT NAME. These details often make the difference between a design that works and one that doesn't. Place your text in this position. To achieve the same look, choose a similar font. $3.00

PRODUCT NAME. To match the overall page design, choose a clip art image of roughly the same weight and density, and duplicate its positioning and proportion to the other elements on the page. $4.00

PRODUCT NAME. These details often make the difference between a design that works and one that doesn't. Place your text in this position. To achieve the same look, choose a similar font. $5.00

PRODUCT NAME. To match the overall page design, choose a clip art image of roughly the same weight and density, and duplicate its positioning and proportion to the other elements on the page. $6.00

PRODUCT NAME. These details often make the difference between a design that works and one that doesn't. Place your text in this position. To achieve the same look, choose a similar $7.0

Sampler Café
MENU

Be on the lookout for pictures within pictures. This cover is a detail cropped from a larger painting, and the image printed inside is a detail from the cover.

93

Multimedia Presentation Clip art is not just for printing on paper.

It works equally as well in slide and overhead presentations, videotape productions, or in this case, to illustrate a computer multimedia program.

The example shows how a restaurant association might market its members. The program could be displayed in a kiosk or distributed on CD-ROM. The introductory screen offers the title, version date, the sponsor's name, and a few teaser questions.

94

Opposite: Wine bottle and glass–from Iconomics Stock and Custom Images. © 1995 Iconomics. All rights reserved.

Hand–from Just Hands by CMCD. © 1995 PhotoDisc Inc. All rights reserved.

Book–from Altemus Cuts Two. © 1995 Altemus Creative Services. All rights reserved.

Looking for something different? Try combining several images and illustration styles in a single composition.

95

Newsletter Introducing the un-newsletter.

It has no masthead. Instead, the headline for the lead story takes center stage. Two large clip art images dominate the layout: a border on the cover and a central image for the inside spread.

The example demonstrates how a church might use the layout to publish monthly news. The bar above the headline names the church and the month of publication. The pastor's letter begins on the front and could continue inside.

For your version, you could change the cover artwork each month or use it as a permanent part of your visual identity.

The page-two lead is boxed and illustrated with a clip art image. Page three features a calendar. The stories continue on the top two-thirds of the back page (not shown). The bottom third is reserved for mailing information. The final piece is folded in half and mailed.

Opposite: Marbled paper–from the Electronic Clipper Service. © 1995 Dynamic Graphics Inc. All rights reserved.

Crayons–from Award Clips. © 1995 Baudville Inc. All rights reserved.

THE SAMPLER CHURCH · JULY 1999

THE POWER OF GOOD

Pastor's Letter

Place your text in this position. To achieve the same look, choose a similar font and duplicate the size, spacing, and alignment. To match the overall page design, choose a clip art image of roughly the same weight and density, and duplicate its positioning and proportion to the other elements on the page. These details often make the difference between a design that works and one that doesn't. Place your text in this position. To achieve the same look, choose a similar font and duplicate the size, spacing, and alignment.

To match the overall page design, choose a clip art image of roughly the same weight and density, and duplicate its positioning and proportion to the other elements on the page. These details often make the difference between a design that works and one that doesn't. Place your text in this position. To achieve the same look, choose a similar font and duplicate the size, spacing, and alignment. To match the overall page design, choose a clip art image of roughly the same weight and density, and duplicate its positioning and proportion to the other elements on the page. These details often make the difference between a design that works and one that doesn't.

Place your text in this position. To achieve the same look, choose a similar font and duplicate the size, spacing, and alignment. To match the overall page design, choose a clip art image of roughly the same weight and density, and duplicate its positioning and proportion to the other elements on the page. These details often make the difference between a design that works and one that doesn't. Place your text in this position. To achieve the same look, choose.— *Dr. Roger M. Example*

The box around the crayons is a series of lines that end at the edge of each crayon. This creates an illusion that the crayons are sitting on the page.

Package Insert New technology has put the production of audio and video programs within the reach of a new wave of creative minds.

But far fewer folks will see or hear your production if your package doesn't reflect the quality of your message.

This example shows how a university might distribute an orientation to the school's athletic program. The cover includes the title and a stand-alone image.

The cover title is repeated on the spine and the cover art is duplicated inside along with the name of the speaker, the tape's running time, and the required contact information.

Customizable audio cassette, CD-ROM, and videotape labels and packaging are widely available.

98

Opposite: Basketball–from the Sports category of the Oswego Illustrated Archives. © 1995 Oswego Company. All rights reserved.

Sampler University Basketball

B
b a LL

Program

Sampler University Basketball

B
b a LL

Program
An introduction
by Head Coach
Herb Example

Running time: 64:00 minutes
For more information contact
Public Affairs Office
Sampler University
Your City, ST 12345-6789
987-654-3210

The Sampler University
Basketball Program
with Head Coach, Herb Example

Running time: 64:00 minutes
© 1999 Sampler University

Good design does not need to be complex. At times, a single object and an interesting type composition is all that's necessary to tell the story.

Package Label Bags, bottles, boxes, cans, jars, tubes, and other vessels emblazoned with your label or tag are among the most impressive projects you can produce from the desktop.

This project, unlike the others, was not designed for *Clip Art Crazy*. I thought, instead, that you should see how the Charles S. Anderson Design Company uses its own CSA Archive images to produce products and packaging. (For the full story, see the CSA Archive Company chapter beginning on page 195.)

These industrial-strength cans embellished with simple round labels are one example of an enormous selection of blank packaging available from industrial product suppliers.

One good source for blank packaging is Consolidated Plastics Company Inc., 8181 Darrow Rd., Twinsburg, OH 44087 USA, Voice: 800-362-1000, 216-425A-3900; Fax: 216-425-3333.

Opposite: Miscellaneous images–from the CSA Archive. © 1995 CSA Archive. All rights reserved.

The CSA Archive markets a line of products designed using their marvelous stock cuts. Among them is this boxed set of cloisonne pins. Crazy.

101

Pad If you find yourself scribbling notes to colleagues and clients on full-size stationery, this project is for you.

Pads are a more casual, less expensive way to send your message. Three examples:

A physician might use a blood pressure cuff to create a pad for jotting down notes to patients. A high school teacher uses a "NOW READ THIS!" loudspeaker. And a banker uses a dollar bill background on a pad for writing notes to clients.

You'll be surprised how economically a commercial printer can print and assemble pads.

102

Martin B. Sampler, M.D.

Sampler Heart Center
11475 Example Trace
Your City, ST 12345
Voice 987-654-3210
Fax 987-654-3210

NOW READ THIS!

Mr. Larry V. Sampler
Example High School
123 Example Walk
Your City, ST 12345
Voice 987-654-3210
Fax 987-654-3210

Though the original image of George Washington was quite bold, adjusting the tone has transformed it into a faint but effective background.

103

David M. Sampler

ExampleBank
123 Example Lakes
Your City, ST 12345-6789
Voice 987-654-3210
Fax 987-654-3210
Email abc@def.com

Pocket Folder A carefully chosen illustration is a bold statement about who you are.

A pocket folder is an ideal way to make that statement. The example shows a folder that might be used by a law firm to pitch new accounts or to present papers. The cover features an illustration printed in a shade and color that keeps the name of the firm as the focus. The name, address, and phone number are repeated on the inside flap and back cover.

All pocket folders are not created equal. There are literally hundreds of possible combinations—large and small folders, with various size pockets, featuring everything from simple cutouts for mounting your business card to built-in, detachable rotary cards.

A company that specializes in printing folders can save you big bucks because they already have the costly dies used to cut the final folder. This example was printed by Gentile Brothers Folder Factory, 116-A High St., P.O. Box 429, Edinburg, VA 22824 USA, Voice: 800-296-4321, 540-984-8852; Fax: 540-984-9699.

Opposite: Justice–from Images of Women Volume 1. © 1995 Harter Image Archives. All rights reserved.

Does your artwork need explaining? The caption on the lower left cover reads: "Justice holds a sword to symbolize the power of the law and scales to represent impartiality."

105

Pop-Up Card The whole is greater than the sum of it's parts.

Two images plus a simple pop-up turn a flat card into a fancy, 3-D message.

The example is an invitation to the opening of a business park. The cover headline teases the payoff on the panel below the artwork. One illustration covers the middle panel, a second fits on the pop-up panel within it.

An invitation typically includes the name of the host or organization, the day, date, and hour, the location, phone number, and, if necessary, an R.S.V.P.

Your local commercial printer can print, score, and die-cut the card. The 4-by-5 $^{1}/_{2}$-inch folded card fits snugly in an A2-style envelope.

106

Opposite: Birdbath, town—from Iconomics Stock and Custom Images. © 1995 Iconomics. All rights reserved.

How else but with clip art and stock art can you buy the skills of such talented people, for so little money, and use the substantial results to your own benefit?

Postcard Postcards in an e-mail, overnight, Internet world? Yes! Personalized postcards are a great way to handle your not-urgent communications and tangible proof of your interest and concern. Use them for notes, greetings, and for answering those "I'll find out and get back with you" questions without a protracted phone call.

The examples show both the mailing and message sides of two designs. The illustrations symbolize the business of the sender—a globe for a travel consultant and figures studying a globe for a market researcher.

Include the same information you would print on your business card: your company name and return address on the mailing side, and your name, title, phone and e-mail numbers, and a description of your business on the message side.

108

Opposite: Globe–from Everyday Objects 3 by CMCD. © 1995 PhotoDisc Inc. All rights reserved.

Figures with globe–from the Primatives Fontek DesignFont. © 1995 Letraset USA. All rights reserved.

Sampler Travel

11475 Example Bridge
Your City, State 12345-6789

Old Glory

USA G
For U.S. addresses only

Peter Sampler

Corporate
Travel Specialist
Voice 987.654.3210
Fax 987.654.3210
E-Mail abc@def.com

from
Betty Sampler
Vice President of
Example Research...
Consumer & Industrial
Market Research
Voice 987.654.3210
Fax 987.654.3210
E-Mail abc@def.com

Sampler Research
123 Example Park
7th Floor, Suite 123
Your City,
State 12345-6789

*With so many images to
choose from, it's easy to
overdo it. Some projects
work best with a simple
layout and a single image.*

109

Poster Clip art ten times normal size speaks with a different voice.

This poster is roughly 15 inches by 19 inches. At that size, an ordinary image becomes interesting and an extraordinary image becomes downright stunning.

Just about any desktop publishing service bureau can print a page that is up to 18 inches wide by as long as you care to make it. Companies that specialize in oversize digital prints (you'll find their ads in the back of the desktop publishing magazines) can print billboard-size images!

Some software programs allow you to "tile" a page at a larger size than a typical printer can handle. This poster, for example, was created on a standard 8 $\frac{1}{2}$-by-11-inch page, then printed at 175 percent as four separate tiles. The tiles were trimmed out and assembled into a finished poster measuring roughly 15 inches by 19 inches."

Opposite: Moon–from the Holidays Set. © 1995 Art Parts. All rights reserved.

Bird, nest–from the Nature/Environment Set. © 1995 Art Parts. All rights reserved.

If you can't find a fitting image, try building one. In this case two clip art images were used—the bird and nest to represent the "parent" and the moon to represent "night."

111

Parent's Night

Sampler Elementary School, Tuesday, May 25th, 7-9 p.m.

Proposal If the words "proposal" and "report" don't fill you with desktop passion, you're not alone.

The do's and don'ts of technical document design have reduced these popular formats to nothing more than visual pablum.

But all is not lost. While structure is relevant, it should subordinate the design, not dominate it. Pages don't have to be vertical, paper doesn't have to be white, and illustrations don't have to be boring.

The example shows how a real estate company might present a new property to investors. The cover illustration is printed in a light tone to ensure that the proposal title is the focal point. The images on the text pages occupy the same area as the title on the cover. For your version, repeat a single image on every inside page or use a different image for each section of the report.

112

Opposite: Landscapes–from the Electronic Clipper Service. © 1995 Dynamic Graphics Inc. All rights reserved.

Sampler Trace Technology Park

A proposal by Example Properties
March 16, 1999

Place your text in this position. To achieve the same look, choose a similar font and duplicate the size, spacing, and alignment. To match the overall page design, choose a clip art image of roughly the same weight and density, and duplicate its positioning and proportion to the other elements on the page. These details often make the difference between a design that works and one that doesn't.

Place your text in this position. To achieve the same look, choose a similar font and duplicate the size, spacing, and alignment.

To match the overall page design, choose a clip art image of roughly the same weight and density, and duplicate its positioning and proportion to the other elements on the page. These details often make the difference between a design that works and one that doesn't. Place your text in this position. To achieve the same look, choose a similar font and duplicate the size, spacing, and alignment. To match the overall page design, choose a clip art image of roughly the same weight and density, and duplicate its positioning and proportion to the other elements on the page. These details often make the difference between a design that works and one that doesn't. Place your text in this position. To achieve the same look, choose a similar font and duplicate the size, spacing, and alignment. To match the overall page design, choose a clip art image of roughly the same weight and density, and duplicate its positioning and proportion to the other elements on the page. These details often make the difference between a design that works and one that doesn't. Place your text in this position. To achieve the same look, choose a similar font and duplicate the size, spacing, and alignment. To match the overall page design, choose a clip art image of roughly the same weight and density, and duplicate its positioning and proportion to the other elements on the page. These details often make the difference between a design that works and one that doesn't. Place your text in this position. To achieve the same look, choose a similar font and duplicate the size, spacing, and

Projected Occupancy Rates

A proposal by Example Properties
March 16, 1999

Clip art is one way to bring a sense of reality to concepts and products that are still on the drawing board.

113

Roll-Fold Brochure If you've got more products or services than space, a roll-fold brochure could be the answer.

This pocket-size version gives you a whopping ten panels to work with—five on each side. The flat size is roughly 13 $\frac{5}{8}$ inches by 5 $\frac{1}{4}$ inches. The cover and back cover panels are the same width—2 $\frac{3}{4}$ inches. To allow for the roll-fold; each succeeding panel is approximately $\frac{1}{16}$-inch shorter than the one that precedes it.

Your version could be any size and number of panels the printing press can accommodate.

114

Opposite: Cats, dogs–from Dick & Jane and Return of Dick and Jane by Mark van Bronkhorst (product in font format). Dog drinking from toilet–from MvB Archive Scratch 'n Sniff by Georgia Panagiotopoulos (product in EPS/WMF formats). Cat with kittens–from MvB Archive CatHaus by Georgia Panagiotopoulos (product in EPS/WMF formats). © 1995 MvB Design. All rights reserved.

Does your typeface match your illustration? This typeface is as playful as the artwork around it. Choose the image first, then match a typeface to it.

115

Rotary Card There are few things more frustrating than meeting a prospect who just bought your competitor's product or service—not because it was better, but because they happened upon it first.

Successful marketing requires more than a convincing offer—it requires a convincing and timely offer.

If you can capture a spot in your prospect's rotary file, you have a far better chance of getting the call when a need arises. The example demonstrates how a catering company might do it. The image signals, at a glance, that the topic is food. In addition to the name, a description of services, and the obvious contact information—this card goes so far as to solicit a phone call by asking, "May we fax our current menu?"

Your version might also include hours of operation, your e-mail and Internet addresses, and directions to your place of business.

Laser printer compatible rotary cards like the one shown here are available at most office supply stores and through the mail. If you want a more durable version with a tab, have your artwork printed on a plastic rotary card by Continental Plastic Card Co., 3651 NW 120th Ave., Coral Springs, FL 33065 USA, Voice: 800-543-0670, 305-753-0670; Fax: 305-341-3479.

116

Opposite: Sandwich–from Metro Subscription Service. © 1995 Metro Creative Graphics Inc. All rights reserved.

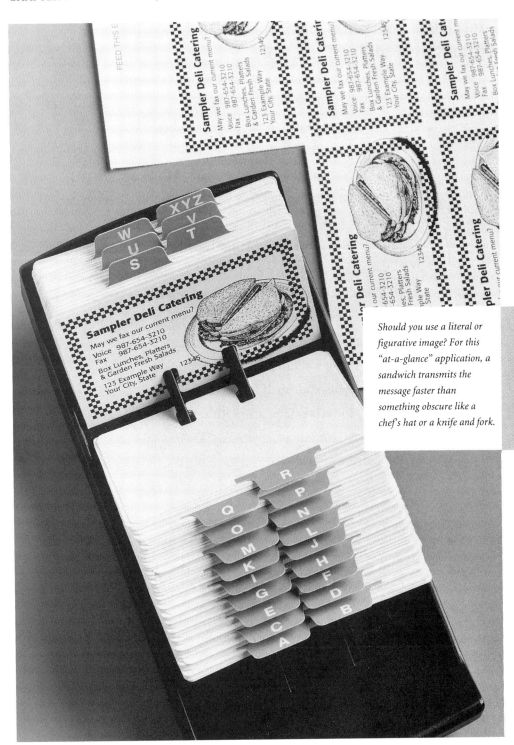

Should you use a literal or figurative image? For this "at-a-glance" application, a sandwich transmits the message faster than something obscure like a chef's hat or a knife and fork.

117

Shelf Sign Some estimates say over 50 percent of buying decisions are made inside the store.

So it stands to reason that point-of-purchase incentives such as special pricing, product information, or reasons to buy, can play a key role in moving merchandise.

The example shows how a retailer might use a bit of self-deprecating humor to advertise a "Manager's SPECIAL." This version is 5 $\frac{1}{2}$ inches by 8 $\frac{1}{2}$ inches—a half sheet of a standard 11-by-8 $\frac{1}{2}$-inch sheet of paper.

Your version could list product features, product comparisons, or it could cross-merchandise other products (such as "don't forget the batteries"). You might print the prices in place or you could duplicate a supply of signs with a blank area for entering offers by hand.

If you want to see some other interesting devices for displaying your shelf signs, get a copy of the retail merchandising products catalog from Russell & Miller Inc., 12342 Bell Ranch Dr., Santa Fe Springs, CA 90670-3356 USA, Voice: 800-231-9600; Fax: 800-527-2488, 310-941-1654.

Opposite: Blackboard–from Megatoons. © 1995 Creative Media Services. All rights reserved.

Look beyond the obvious use of an image. This cartoon of a professor works equally as well as a store manager.

Shopping Bag Around the turn of the century, merchants hired agents to walk the streets wearing "sandwich board" signs to advertise their wares.

The modern equivalent is the shopping bag. For a few pennies per bag, your customers could be broadcasting your name and message every time they walk out your door.

But bags are not for retailers only. Your version could be anything from a trade show giveaway to gift wrapping.

Bags are made from all kinds of materials and come in every imaginable shape, color, and size. The example was printed for a bag from Elman Labels and Paper Products, 2311 Perkins Pl., Silver Spring, MD 20910 USA, Voice: 800-442-2247, 301-588-8292; Fax: 301-587-4153.

120

Opposite: Sports–from Simple Silhouettes-Volume 19. © 1995 Image Club Graphics Inc. All rights reserved.

What looks like one complex image is actually ten simple silhouettes arranged within a border.

121

Signature Card One essential element for building relationships is the sharing of information.

A signature card is a handsome way to attach your business card to information you send to colleagues and clients—your marketing materials, a proposal or report, a product sample, or, perhaps, a photocopy of a pertinent newspaper article.

The example demonstrates how a financial consultant might pass along a prospectus to an interested client. This version is 5 $\frac{1}{2}$ inches by 8 $\frac{1}{2}$ inches—a half sheet of a standard 11-by-8 $\frac{1}{2}$-inch sheet of paper. A flap, roughly 3 inches long, holds the card in place. It features an illustration to broadcast the topic, a generic headline, and slots for inserting a business card.

122

Opposite: Money–from Metro Subscription Service. © 1995 Metro Creative Graphics Inc. All rights reserved.

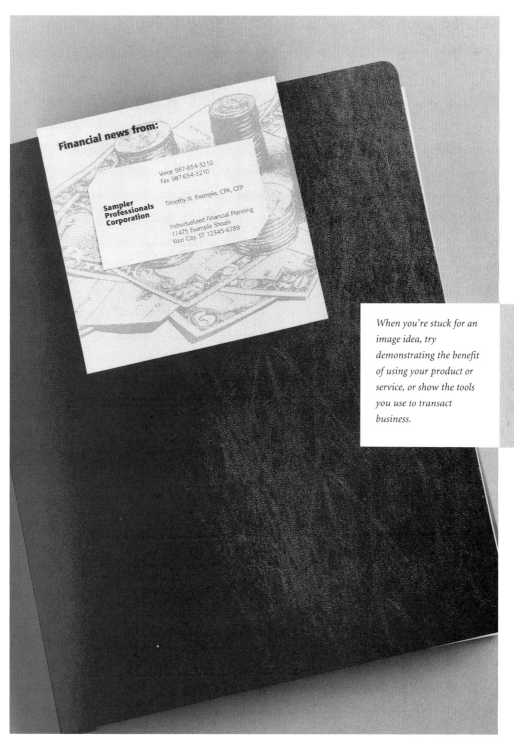

Financial news from:

Voice 987-654-3210
Fax 987-654-3210

**Sampler
Professionals
Corporation**

Timothy N. Example, CPA, CFP

Individualized Financial Planning
11475 Example Shoals
Your City, ST 12345-6789

When you're stuck for an image idea, try demonstrating the benefit of using your product or service, or show the tools you use to transact business.

123

Small-Space Ad As with any of the projects in this chapter, a successful ad campaign requires all the basics—the right product, benefit, offer, timing, audience, media, and exposure.

A full-size ad obviously gets better exposure, but beyond that, a small-space ad can be equally effective.

The example shows how a training company might advertise classes for novice computer users. This simple layout allows the illustration and headline to do the lion's share of the work.

Opposite: Computer–from the ClickArt On the Job Cartoons portfolio. © 1995 T/Maker Company. All rights reserved worldwide.

Conquer computerphobia

Place your text in this position. To achieve the same look, choose a similar font and duplicate the size, spacing, and alignment. To match the overall page design, choose a clip art image of roughly the same weight and density, and dupli- cate its positioning. Call 654-3210.

123 Example Ville, Suite 456, Fax 654-3210

SamplerTech Training

Watch for dated illustrations. The computer model and clothing styles represented here are generic enough that this image should be useful today and in the foreseeable future.

125

Sticker If you doubt the value of embellishing your packages and mail with something as simple as an eye-catching sticker, take a look at the materials you are competing with.

Overnight and priority packages use bold graphics and words to create a sense of urgency on the part of the recipient and the people who handle your package along the way.

Laser printer compatible stickers like these are available at most office supply stores and through the mail in many different sizes and colors.

Opposite: Clock–from the A*I Eclectic font. © 1995 Alphabets Inc. All rights reserved.

126

Globe–from Volume 7 - Circular Designs of Design Elements-A Digital Reference. © 1995 Ultimate Symbol Inc. All rights reserved.

Sun–from Volume 1 - Stars Suns Moons Zodiac of Design Elements-A Digital Reference. © 1995 Ultimate Symbol Inc. All rights reserved.

Book–from Altemus Cuts Two. © 1995 Altemus Creative Services. All rights reserved.

Think internationally. If your materials are going beyond your own borders, it's important to use words and images that speak to a global audience.

127

T-Shirt Ad specialties—T-shirts, hats, calendars, pens, and so on—compel prospects to call or visit.

They reward customers for ordering, communicate a heartfelt thank you, serve as a team and employee motivator, and are a popular way to plant your name and grow it.

The value of clip art on T-shirts is obvious. It is a simple way to transmit a quality image with a minimum investment. All it takes is an appropriate image and a few words of type to make it yours.

The example shows the type of T-shirt a production company might use as a perk for clients or to outfit its staff.

Need quality-imprinted items like this shirt? Call HA•LO Marketing & Promotions, 1001 E. Main St. #917, Richmond, VA 23219 USA, Voice: 800-474-4256 (ask for the Value Line Dept.), 804-644-0455; Fax: 804-644-0458.

128

Opposite: Prop man–from the Entertainment Set.
© 1995 Art Parts. All rights reserved.

Check each clip art company's legalese. Although creating a T-shirt for your softball team may be perfectly acceptable, shirts intended for resale typically require an additional fee.

129

Table Tent Who among us doesn't enjoy seeing his or her name in print? A table tent is one of the simple amenities that makes a meeting memorable.

They help you arrange seating and aid participants in identifying the names and affiliation of their colleagues.

The example is folded from a standard-size heavy sheet of 8 ¹/₂-by-11-inch paper. The page is divided into thirds, minus a quarter-inch flap for gluing or taping. Use a straight edge and a letter opener to score (crease) the folds.

130

Opposite: Ornament–from Volume 4-Arabesque Ornaments. © 1994, 1995 Aridi Computer Graphics Inc.

This ornament is a small piece of a larger image. It's not unusual to find many useful parts to separate or crop from a larger or more complex illustration.

131

Chapter 5

Just for Fun

Bookmark Think of your bookmark as an oversize business card or a miniature brochure.

Use it as an inexpensive handout or leave-behind to promote your products and services.

The example on the left, for an animal clinic, forgoes a headline and relies instead on the images to grab the reader's attention and pull him or her into the message.

The second example demonstrates how a library communicates its hours of operation, address, phone number, and a bit of history.

For your version, use a clip art illustration to establish the mood, a headline and/or text to do some selling, and the balance of space to provide your reader with a call to action. Repeat the same design on the second side or use the added space to expand your message.

134

Opposite: Doctor, dog, reading–from Illustrated Stock Cuts. © 1995 Daniel Pelavin. All rights reserved.

Simple, well-designed images like these are often the most difficult to create and the hardest to find. A talented illustrator can reduce a concept to its essence without sacrificing its personality.

135

Cake Stake Forget the candles and the fancy decorations—you can say it all with the latest in "high-tech culinary signage."

The football player is printed on laser paper and glued to a second, heavier sheet to create a rigid sign. The stake is a craft stick from a local arts and crafts store. This example was trimmed out using an art knife, but yours could be a simple rectangle. (Note: Be sure you have a good, clean laser print; the last thing I want is toner on my cake!)

Opposite: Football –from ArtSource Volume Three-Sports. © 1995 Youth Specialties Inc. All rights reserved.

You can punctuate the shape of an image by printing it on a screened background.

Clock A clip art clock may sound a little loony, but it does, in fact, make an impressive gift, decoration, or in this case, a unique sign.

You'll find plastic, battery-powered clocks like these in most home products and office supply superstores. They cost less than $10 and the 6 $^3/_4$-inch face can be trimmed easily from a standard 8 $^1/_2$-by-11-inch sheet of paper.

The process is easy. You disassemble the clock (most hands pull off easily) and use the existing face as a template for locating the hour marks. Print your design on a sheet of laser paper, trim out the circle with an art knife, and attach it to the clock using spray glue. Voilà—a clock worth watching.

138

In some cases, the illustration styles from different clip art collections match almost exactly.

139

Coloring Sheet A coloring sheet is a simple way to keep little hands busy while you attend to the business at hand.

And object-oriented clip art is a particularly easy way to create interesting pictures to color. A copy of the object-oriented image, shown at the bottom left of the sheet, was opened in a drawing software program. The color fills were then removed leaving a wire frame, perfect for coloring.

Your version could include text with facts about the image, a story, or some interesting details about your organization.

Opposite: Puffin–from the Wildlife volume. © 1995 ARISEN Corp. All rights reserved.

With draw or paint software programs, you can add or delete colors and shapes or use the pieces and parts of illustrations to create your own compositions.

141

Exhibit Some clip art is even suitable for framing.

An apt illustration punctuates a setting in much the same way that it amplifies a newsletter page.

You'll find a sizable selection of ready-made frames and mats to fit 8 ½-by-11-inch or smaller images at most arts and crafts stores. Buy the frames and mats first, then size and print your illustrations to fit. The framed initial *M* might be used as a gift for a newborn.

142

Opposite: Fish, owl, mirror–from the Past-Tints Sampler Edition. © 1995 Periwinkle Software. All rights reserved.

Much of the best clip art is
not created using a
computer at all. It is
created in a conventional
medium, then digitized for
use on the computer.

143

Invitation With the right images and some creative cuts and folds, you can produce paper sculpture.

The example shows how a museum might use water and shell images as backdrops for an invitation. The unfolded sheets (top) show the die-cuts necessary.

An invitation typically includes the name of the host or organization, the day, date, hour, location, phone number, and, if necessary, an R.S.V.P.

144

Opposite: Shell–from Everyday Objects 1 by CMCD. © 1995 PhotoDisc Inc. All rights reserved.

Water drops–from the Electronic Clipper Service. © 1995 Dynamic Graphics Inc. All rights reserved.

Try using an image as a puzzle. The portion of the shell revealed in the folded invitation shows just enough to get the reader to explore further.

145

Mail Art Envelope While you might view an envelope as nothing more than a means of delivery, mail art aficionados consider it a medium of expression.

Mail art is the craft of drawing or rubber stamping elaborate combinations of images and patterns on letterheads and envelopes—whole books have been devoted to the subject.

With electronic clip art, you can create the high-tech equivalent to traditional mail art. To create your version, find an envelope style you want to use, carefully pull it apart, and use the flat sheet as a template for laying out your page. Print your finished design, cut it into envelope form, and glue it together.

If you're curious about mail art in general and rubber stamps in particular, sign up for a subscription to Rubberstampmadness, P.O. Box 610 Corvallis, OR 97339 USA, Voice: 503-752-0075, Fax: 503-752-5475.

Opposite: Ornaments–from Volumes 3-Historical Ornaments, Patterns & Frames, Volume 4-Arabesque Ornaments, Volume 5-Arabesque Borders. © 1994, 1995 Aridi Computer Graphics Inc.

Try printing your project on a variety of paper colors and textures—they often have a dramatic effect on the end result.

147

Milk Bottle Cap If you haven't heard of milk bottle cap mania, you don't have school-age kids or know anyone who does.

Milk bottle caps are used as playing pieces for games, and, perhaps more important, they are traded like baseball cards. Though the initial craze has subsided, the caps remain an easy, entertaining project for schools, churches, clubs, and scout troops.

To create your version, print your designs on round labels and attach them to existing caps, or go to your local toy store and buy—a device designed for this very purpose,—the "Milkcap Maker" from Cap Toys Inc.

Opposite: Lightbulb–from Everyday Objects 2 by CMCD. © 1995 PhotoDisc Inc. All rights reserved.

148

Saw blade–from the A*I Eclectic font. © 1995 Alphabets Inc. All rights reserved.

Sumo wrestling–from Horny Dave by Georgia Panagiotopoulos (product in font format). © 1995 MvB Design. All rights reserved.

Television–from Fabulous Fifties-Volume 21. © 1995 Image Club Graphics Inc. All rights reserved.

Kids love visual language. Artwork personalized with their name or the name of their organization is always a hit.

149

Ornament Here's a new variation of an old theme—the paper chain you created as a kid.

The images are font symbols printed alternately in positive and reverse. You can create several different combinations, then copy, paste, and repeat them down the sheet. Print as many copies as necessary on a variety of paper colors and have a pasting party.

Opposite: Christmas tree, church, holly, piñata, Santa Claus, star, stocking–from the Celebrations Fontek DesignFont. © 1995 Letraset USA. All rights reserved.

One of the easiest ways to customize a clip art image is to change colors, use shades of gray, or reverse it on a dark background.

151

Stationery Every desktop publisher deserves his or her own personal stationery.

The examples are Monarch-size 8 ¼-by-10-inch pages, decorated with simple wallpaper patterns of font images. The back of each sheet features a solid pattern of images; the front of the sheet is used as the writing surface.

Match your letterhead to a color-coordinated 7 ½-by-3 ⅞-inch Monarch size envelope.

152

Opposite: Ram–from the Petroglyph font. © 1995 Judith Sutcliffe: The Electric Typographer. All rights reserved.

Clocks–from the A*I Eclectic font. © 1995 Alphabets Inc. All rights reserved.

Grapes–from the A*I Apple Wine font. © 1995 Alphabets Inc. All rights reserved.

JUDITH SAMPLER
123 Example Lane, Your City, State 12345-6789
987.654.3210

TRAVIS SAMPLER
11475 Example Branch, Your City, State 12345-6789
987-654-3210

SAMPLER VINEYARDS
11475 Example Branch, Your City, State 12345-6789
987.654.3210

Add interest with subtle details—instead of a simple pattern of rams, add one rebel facing in the opposite direction. Instead of using one clock face, use all twelve hour positions.

153

Stencil Adding depth and dimension to an image is another way to make it uniquely yours.

This, believe it or not, is a window shutter. Simple, bold icons such as these make striking ornaments. You can paint them by means of a stencil, cut them out of the shutter, or cut a design from wood and attach it in relief.

The sun and swan are roughly 4 $^1\!/_2$ inches on a 15 inch shutter. To create your version, select and print out a symbol with reverse white lines to locate the center. From the print, you can create a stencil and paint the design or transfer the image to the shutter and trim it out with a scroll saw.

With a little imagination, you can use clip art to create all kinds of unique bric-a-brac for your home's exterior and interior.

154

Opposite: Sun—from Volume 1 - Stars Suns Moons Zodiac of Design Elements—A Digital Reference. © 1995 Ultimate Symbol Inc. All rights reserved.

Swan—from Volume 3 - Pictorial Symbols of Design Elements—A Digital Reference. © 1995 Ultimate Symbol Inc. All rights reserved.

Don't confine your thinking to what other folks use images for.

155

Wrapping Paper Wrapping paper is a wonderfully simple way to use images that you love but can't find any other use for.

The examples demonstrate the use of a single image large and small, and an image combined with a proverb.

Create your version by repeating the image across a standard-size page. Print as many pages as you need to cover the gift, lay them face down on a flat surface and run strips of tape across the seams. You can add extra pizzazz by printing each sheet on a different color.

156

Opposite: Hedgehog–from the Wildlife Accents volume. © 1995 ARISEN Corp. All rights reserved.

Leaf–from Altemus Cuts Two. © 1995 Altemus Creative Services. All rights reserved.

For a totally different effect, try printing a series of complementary, full-page images and assembling them into a single large sheet.

157

Part III

Clip Art Catalog

Clip Art Catalog The companies listed here represent a sea change in the clip art market.

They are the standard-bearers, the niche marketers, the rebels, the serious minded, and a company or two that is proud to be a few cards short of a full deck. Together they and others are reinventing the concept of clip art.

The 20 companies featured in the chapters that follow did not solicit space or coverage here; rather, they were actively pursued for this project from the author's A-list of companies. Happily, all but one or two invited guests came to the party. They are, of course, not the only companies that create great illustrations. The Source List in Chapter 1 gives you some idea of the scope of what is available.

All but a few of the 500 images cataloged here were hand picked by the author from the tens of thousands of available images. The general criteria for selecting the 25 samples that represent each company were to demonstrate the quality of each company's art and the diversity of their subject matter. The result is an unprecedented sampling of the market and an extraordinary collection of images on CD-ROM.

On the opening pages of each chapter is an overview of the company, its products, and the people who make it work. The remainder of the pages catalog the images by file name and type. File names begin with a three-letter abbreviation of the company name, a two-digit number that corresponds to the listing, and a single letter that tells you at a glance whether the image is black and white (B); color (C); or that it includes two images, one color and one black and white (M). These chapters serve as a quick reference for finding just the right image.

Before you use any file, be sure to read and heed the text file included in each company's directory—it begins with READ and ends with .WRI. The file includes the company's license agreement, which explains when and how you can use the images, along with any other information the company elected to provide.

For technical tips and instructions on using the *Clip Art Crazy CD-ROM* see CD-ROM Instructions on page 360.

Chapter 6

Aridi
Computer
Graphics

Aridi Art Images

Aridi Art Images Call it visual poetry—exquisite borders, initials, ornaments, and fluid calligraphy.

To create it, you need an understanding of fine art, solid technical skills, and no small amount of talent. Marwan Aridi, the president and founder of Aridi Computer Graphics, has an abundance of all three.

Aridi studied design and Arabic calligraphy in his native Lebanon and completed his graduate studies in graphic design and advertising in the United States. He uses his educated eye to search everything from manuscripts and carvings to tiles and textiles for images that fit his vision for the Aridi collection. Some of the representations are faithful re-creations of ancient motifs, some are interpretations, and others are Aridi's own designs.

The Olde World Borders collection, for example, features elements created in Arabesque, Art Deco, Celtic, and Victorian styles. You'll find filigreed columns with faces, delicate grape-vines, and symmetrical ribbon work. Aridi's Initial Caps volumes were inspired by medieval religious manuscripts in which artisans used ornate letterforms to highlight the opening pages of the gospels. Those styles include everything from an interpretation of a gothic alphabet to a few of Aridi's own modern entries.

In addition to the kind of images shown here, Aridi publishes Arabic Initial Caps & Fonts and Arabic Calligraphy Art titles that feature sayings and verses from the Koran, many presented on exquisitely complex backgrounds.

All images from the full Aridi collections come in both

164

Page 163 and above: Ornaments–from Volume 3–Historical Ornaments, Patterns & Frames. © 1994, 1995 Aridi Computer Graphics Inc. All rights reserved.

color and black and white in a variety of file formats. The detail of the files is extraordinary. Even the bitmapped versions of the files are meticulously edited, pixel by pixel, for maximum effect.

The *Clip Art Crazy CD-ROM* includes 25 Aridi Art Images in a directory labeled: ARIDI. The files are saved as both PostScript (EPS) files for use with PostScript printers and as Windows Bitmap (BMP) for use with non-PostScript printers. The file labeled READARI.WRI (in the same directory) includes the company's license agreement, which explains when and how you can use the images, along with any other information the company elected to provide.

For more information see Appendix page 341 or contact:

Aridi Computer Graphics Inc.

P.O. Box 797702, Dallas, TX 75379 USA

Voice: 800-755-6441, 214-404-9171; Fax: 214-404-9172

The graphics shown on the pages of Clip Art Crazy *and included on the* Clip Art Crazy CD-ROM *are from Aridi's six-volume collection. © 1994, 1995 Aridi Computer Graphics Inc. All rights reserved. For Aridi copyright and licensing restrictions, please see the READARI.WRI file on the* Clip Art Crazy CD-ROM.

165

Ornament–from Volume 4–Arabesque Ornaments. © 1994, 1995 Aridi Computer Graphics Inc. All rights reserved.

File name(s):
ARI_01_B.EPS
ARI_01_C.EPS
ARI_01_M.BMP

Initial capital "A"–from Volume 1–Initial Caps–Gothic font. © 1994, 1995 Aridi Computer Graphics Inc. All rights reserved.

File name(s):
ARI_02_B.EPS
ARI_02_C.EPS
ARI_02_M.BMP

Initial capital "B"–from Volume 1–Initial Caps–Gothic font. © 1994, 1995 Aridi Computer Graphics Inc. All rights reserved.

166

File name(s):
ARI_03_B.EPS
ARI_03_C.EPS
ARI_03_M.BMP

Initial capital "A"–from Volume 1–Initial Caps–Regal font. © 1994, 1995 Aridi Computer Graphics Inc. All rights reserved.

File name(s):
ARI_04_B.EPS
ARI_04_C.EPS
ARI_04_M.BMP

Initial capital "B"–from Volume 1–Initial Caps–Regal font. © 1994, 1995 Aridi Computer Graphics Inc. All rights reserved.

File name(s):
ARI_05_B.EPS
ARI_05_C.EPS
ARI_05_M.BMP

Initial capital "A"–from Volume 1–Initial Caps–Wind font. © 1994, 1995 Aridi Computer Graphics Inc. All rights reserved.

Initial capital "A"–from Volume 1–Initial Caps–Wind font. © *1994, 1995 Aridi Computer Graphics Inc. All rights reserved.*

File name(s):
ARI_06_B.EPS
ARI_06_C.EPS
ARI_06_M.BMP

Initial capital "A"–from Volume 2–Initial Caps–Royal font. © *1994, 1995 Aridi Computer Graphics Inc. All rights reserved.*

File name(s):
ARI_07_B.EPS
ARI_07_C.EPS
ARI_07_M.BMP

Initial capital "B"–from Volume 2–Initial Caps–Royal font. © *1994, 1995 Aridi Computer Graphics Inc. All rights reserved.*

File name(s):
ARI_08_B.EPS
ARI_08_C.EPS
ARI_08_M.BMP

167

Initial capital "A"–from Volume 2–Initial Caps–Romant font. © *1994, 1995 Aridi Computer Graphics Inc. All rights reserved.*

File name(s):
ARI_09_B.EPS
ARI_09_C.EPS
ARI_09_M.BMP

Initial capital "B"–from Volume 2–Initial Caps–Romant font. © *1994, 1995 Aridi Computer Graphics Inc. All rights reserved.*

File name(s):
ARI_10_B.EPS
ARI_10_C.EPS
ARI_10_M.BMP

File name(s):
ARI_11_B.EPS
ARI_11_C.EPS
ARI_11_M.BMP

Initial capital "A"–from
Volume 2–Initial
Caps–Napoli font. ©
1994, 1995 Aridi
Computer Graphics Inc.
All rights reserved.

File name(s):
ARI_12_B.EPS
ARI_12_C.EPS
ARI_12_M.BMP

Initial capital "B"–from
Volume 2–Initial
Caps–Napoli font. ©
1994, 1995 Aridi
Computer Graphics Inc.
All rights reserved.

File name(s):
ARI_13_B.EPS
ARI_13_C.EPS
ARI_13_M.BMP

Initial capital "A"–from
Volume 2–Initial
Caps–Lubna font. ©
1994, 1995 Aridi
Computer Graphics Inc.
All rights reserved.

File name(s):
ARI_14_B.EPS
ARI_14_C.EPS
ARI_14_M.BMP

Initial capital "B"–from
Volume 2–Initial
Caps–Lubna font. ©
1994, 1995 Aridi
Computer Graphics Inc.
All rights reserved.

File name(s):
ARI_15_B.BMP
ARI_15_B.EPS
ARI_15_C.BMP
ARI_15_C.EPS

Ornament–from
Volume 3–Historical
Ornaments, Patterns &
Frames. © 1994, 1995
Aridi Computer
Graphics Inc. All rights
reserved.

Ornament–from Volume 3–Historical Ornaments, Patterns & Frames. © 1994, 1995 Aridi Computer Graphics Inc. All rights reserved.	*File name(s):* ARI_16_B.BMP ARI_16_B.EPS ARI_16_C.BMP ARI_16_C.EPS	
Ornament–from Volume 3–Historical Ornaments, Patterns & Frames. © 1994, 1995 Aridi Computer Graphics Inc. All rights reserved.	*File name(s):* ARI_17_B.BMP ARI_17_B.EPS ARI_17_C.BMP ARI_17_C.EPS	
Ornament–from Volume 4–Arabesque Ornaments. © 1994, 1995 Aridi Computer Graphics Inc. All rights reserved.	*File name(s):* ARI_18_B.BMP ARI_18_B.EPS ARI_18_C.BMP ARI_18_C.EPS	
Ornament–from Volume 4–Arabesque Ornaments. © 1994, 1995 Aridi Computer Graphics Inc. All rights reserved. The version shown here is cropped.	*File name(s):* ARI_19_B.BMP ARI_19_B.EPS ARI_19_C.BMP ARI_19_C.EPS	
Ornament–from Volume 4–Arabesque Ornaments. © 1994, 1995 Aridi Computer Graphics Inc. All rights reserved.	*File name(s):* ARI_20_B.BMP ARI_20_B.EPS ARI_20_C.BMP ARI_20_C.EPS	

File name(s):
ARI_21_B.BMP
ARI_21_B.EPS
ARI_21_C.BMP
ARI_21_C.EPS

Ornament–from Volume 5–Arabesque Borders. © 1994, 1995 Aridi Computer Graphics Inc. All rights reserved.

File name(s):
ARI_22_B.BMP
ARI_22_B.EPS
ARI_22_C.BMP
ARI_22_C.EPS

Border–from Volume 5–Arabesque Borders. © 1994, 1995 Aridi Computer Graphics Inc. All rights reserved. The version shown here is cropped.

170

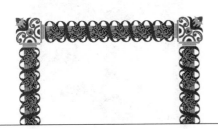

File name(s):
ARI_23_B.BMP
ARI_23_B.EPS
ARI_23_C.BMP
ARI_23_C.EPS

Border–from Volume 5–Arabesque Borders. © 1994, 1995 Aridi Computer Graphics Inc. All rights reserved. The version shown here is cropped.

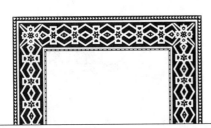

File name(s):
ARI_24_B.EPS
ARI_24_C.BMP
ARI_24_C.EPS

Border–from Volume 6–Olde World Borders. © 1994, 1995 Aridi Computer Graphics Inc. All rights reserved. The version shown here is cropped.

File name(s):
ARI_25_B.EPS
ARI_25_C.BMP
ARI_25_C.EPS

Border–from Volume 6–Olde World Borders. © 1994, 1995 Aridi Computer Graphics Inc. All rights reserved. The version shown here is cropped.

Chapter 7

ARISEN
Corporation

ARROglyphs

ARISEN Corporation is comfortable in its role as small fish in a big pond.

One redeeming aspect of the clip art business is that you can still create a business on a small scale. Though large companies with big mailing lists have an obvious advantage, small companies willing to tackle niche markets can hold their own.

ARISEN is one of those niche players. The company was founded in 1991, under the name ARRO International, by four friends with a common vision. They saw a need for better quality artwork in general and a market that had yet to be tapped.

With their combined skills in traditional and computer graphics, design, and illustration, they created ARROglyphs, the first comprehensive collection of environmental images. These were not just the predictable images, but illustrations as far-reaching as a cutaway of a hydroelectric dam, a depiction of a forest fire, and a series of industry-standard recycling symbols. Titles include Energy, Wildlife, Recycling, Living Planet, Pollution, a picture font titled Wildbits, and others. Their styles encompass woodblock, brush and marker strokes, engravings, and architectural-like diagrams.

ARISEN is not a one-subject company. You can expect future topics to be current and handled with the same incomparable style and attention to detail.

Page 171: Oil well–from the Energy volume. Below: Spray can–from the Pollution volume. © 1995 ARISEN Corp. All rights reserved.

172

The *Clip Art Crazy CD-ROM* includes 25 ARROglyph images in a directory labeled ARISEN. The files are saved as both PostScript (EPS) files for use with PostScript printers and Windows Metafiles (WMF) for use with non-PostScript printers. The file labeled READARS.WRI (in the same directory) includes the company's license agreement, which explains when and how you can use the images, along with any other information the company elected to provide.

For more information see Appendix page 342 or contact:

ARISEN Corporation (formally ARRO International)

P.O. Box 969, Milford, PA 18337 USA

Voice: 800-243-1515, ext. 485, 717-296-5490;

Fax: 717-296-5491

Forest fire–from the Living Planet volume. © 1995 ARISEN Corp. All rights reserved.

173

File name(s):
ARS_01_B.EPS
ARS_01_B.WMF

*Paintbrush and cans–
from the Pollution
volume.
© 1995 ARISEN Corp.
All rights reserved.*

File name(s):
ARS_02_B.EPS
ARS_02_B.WMF

*Dolphin–from the
Living Planet volume. ©
1995 ARISEN Corp. All
rights reserved.*

File name(s):
ARS_03_B.EPS
ARS_03_B.WMF

*Flower–from the Living
Planet volume. © 1995
ARISEN Corp. All rights
reserved.*

174

File name(s):
ARS_04_B.EPS
ARS_04_B.WMF

*Tiger–from the Wildlife
volume. © 1995
ARISEN Corp. All rights
reserved.*

File name(s):
ARS_05_B.EPS
ARS_05_B.WMF

*Ostrich–from the
Wildlife volume. © 1995
ARISEN Corp. All rights
reserved.*

Rhinoceros–from the Wildlife volume. © 1995 ARISEN Corp. All rights reserved.

File name(s):
ARS_06_B.EPS
ARS_06_B.WMF

Paper–from the Recycling volume. © 1995 ARISEN Corp. All rights reserved.

File name(s):
ARS_07_B.EPS
ARS_07_B.WMF

Pop-top can–from the Recycling volume. © 1995 ARISEN Corp. All rights reserved.

File name(s):
ARS_08_B.EPS
ARS_08_B.WMF

Hedgehog–from the Wildlife Accents volume. © 1995 ARISEN Corp. All rights reserved.

File name(s):
ARS_09_B.EPS
ARS_09_B.WMF

Pine cone–from the Wildlife Accents volume. © 1995 ARISEN Corp. All rights reserved.

File name(s):
ARS_10_B.EPS
ARS_10_B.WMF

File name(s):
ARS_11_B.EPS
ARS_11_B.WMF

Paper–from the
Recycling volume.
© 1995 ARISEN Corp.
All rights reserved.

File name(s):
ARS_12_B.EPS
ARS_12_B.WMF

Eagle–from the Living
Planet volume.
© 1995 ARISEN Corp.
All rights reserved.

176

File name(s):
ARS_13_B.EPS
ARS_13_B.WMF

Forest fire–from the
Living Planet volume.
© 1995 ARISEN Corp.
All rights reserved. The
version shown here is
cropped.

File name(s):
ARS_14_B.EPS
ARS_14_B.WMF

Bee–from the Wildlife
Accents volume. © 1995
ARISEN Corp. All rights
reserved.

File name(s):
ARS_15_B.EPS
ARS_15_B.WMF

Lotus flower–from the
Wildlife Accents volume.
© 1995 ARISEN Corp.
All rights reserved.

Puffin–from the Wildlife volume. © 1995 ARISEN Corp. All rights reserved.

File name(s):
ARS_16_C.EPS
ARS_16_C.WMF

Dam–from the Energy volume. © 1995 ARISEN Corp. All rights reserved.

File name(s):
ARS_17_B.EPS
ARS_17_B.WMF

Electricity–from the Energy volume. © 1995 ARISEN Corp. All rights reserved.

File name(s):
ARS_18_B.EPS
ARS_18_B.WMF

177

Cardboard box–from the Recycling volume. © 1995 ARISEN Corp. All rights reserved.

File name(s):
ARS_19_B.EPS
ARS_19_B.WMF

Miner–from the Energy volume. © 1995 ARISEN Corp. All rights reserved.

File name(s):
ARS_20_C.EPS
ARS_20_C.WMF

File name(s):
ARS_21_B.EPS
ARS_21_B.WMF

Gas lamp–from the Energy volume.

File name(s):
ARS_22_B.EPS
ARS_22_B.WMF

Eolian–from the Pollution volume.

178

File name(s):
ARS_23_B.EPS
ARS_23_B.WMF

Waste pipe–from the Pollution volume.

File name(s):
ARS_24_B.EPS
ARS_24_B.WMF

Pipeline–from the Energy volume.

File name(s):
ARS_25_B.EPS
ARS_25_B.WMF

Oil spill–from the Pollution volume.

Chapter 8

Art Parts

Art Parts Sets

Art Parts Ron and Joe of Art Parts are the only guys I know who use a propeller beanie as part of their strategic marketing plan (you get a free one with major purchases).

Ron is the graphic designer, computer jockey, and head writer; Joe is the illustrator (Ron and Joe don't use last names—there may be outstanding warrants). Other players in the Art Parts drama are Carlene, Ron's mom, who contributes a recipe

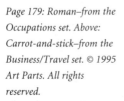

column (recipe column?) to the Art Parts Newsletter, and Noodles the Cat, the feline matriarch (rumor has it Noodles and Carlene have hired a lawyer to squeeze Ron and Joe out).

Suffice it to say, Art Parts, like its creators, have a sense of humor. Joe has chiseled out a planet of people, places, and parts that will bring a smile to the face of anyone who sees them. You'll find everything from practical business illustrations to pure entertainment in sets titled Food, Business/Travel, Occupations, Kids/Education, Nature/Environment, Body Parts, and others.

Ron and Joe have also dabbled in publishing collections by other like-minded illustrators, among them the Relations Set, an adept visual dictionary of human relationships, and the Finance Set, an eclectic view of dollars and sense. You can purchase individual sets, subscribe to a monthly service, or buy the lion's share of the collection on the Art Parts "CD-RON" (oh please!).

180

Page 179: Roman–from the Occupations set. Above: Carrot-and-stick–from the Business/Travel set. © 1995 Art Parts. All rights reserved.

The *Clip Art Crazy CD-ROM* includes 25 Art Parts images in a directory labeled ARTPARTS. The files are saved as Windows Metafiles (WMF) for use with both PostScript and non-PostScript printers. The file labeled READART.WRI (in the same directory) includes the company's license agreement, which explains when and how you can use the images, along with any other information the company elected to provide.

For more information see Appendix page 343 or contact:

Art Parts

P.O. Box 2926, Orange, CA 92669-0926 USA

Voice: 714-771-6754, Fax: 714-633-9617

Left to right: Teacher, daredevil, architect–from the Occupations set. © 1995 Art Parts. All rights reserved.

181

File name(s):
ART_01_B.WMF

Frog–from the Kids/Education set. © 1995 Art Parts. All rights reserved.

File name(s):
ART_02_B.WMF

Santa Claus–from the Holidays Revisited set. © 1995 Art Parts. All rights reserved.

182

File name(s):
ART_03_B.WMF

Meeting–from the Son of Business set. © 1995 Art Parts. All rights reserved.

File name(s):
ART_04_B.WMF

File folder–from the Son of Business set. © 1995 Art Parts. All rights reserved.

File name(s):
ART_05_B.WMF

House–from the Home & Family set. © 1995 Art Parts. All rights reserved.

Vacuum cleaner–from the House Stuff set. © 1995 Art Parts. All rights reserved.

File name(s):
ART_06_B.WMF

Cat–from the Return to Dingbats set. © 1995 Art Parts. All rights reserved.

File name(s):
ART_07_B.WMF

Firecracker–from the Holidays set. © 1995 Art Parts. All rights reserved. The version shown here is cropped.

File name(s):
ART_08_B.WMF

183

Doctor–from the Occupations set. © 1995 Art Parts. All rights reserved.

File name(s):
ART_09_B.WMF

Flying man–from the People set. © 1995 Art Parts. All rights reserved.

File name(s):
ART_10_B.WMF

File name(s):
ART_11_B.WMF

Children–from the Kids/Education set. © 1995 Art Parts. All rights reserved.

File name(s):
ART_12_B.WMF

Face–from the Body Parts set. © 1995 Art Parts. All rights reserved.

184

File name(s):
ART_13_B.WMF

St. Basil Cathedral–from the Goin' Places set. © 1995 Art Parts. All rights reserved.

File name(s):
ART_14_B.WMF

Spaghetti–from the Food set. © 1995 Art Parts. All rights reserved.

File name(s):
ART_15_B.WMF

Crane–from the Son of Animals set. © 1995 Art Parts. All rights reserved.

Tiles–from the Patterns set. © 1995 Art Parts. All rights reserved.

File name(s):
ART_16_B.WMF

Chicken soup–from the Health/Medical set. © 1995 Art Parts. All rights reserved.

File name(s):
ART_17_B.WMF

Movie camera–from the Entertainment set. © 1995 Art Parts. All rights reserved.

File name(s):
ART_18_B.WMF

Ventriloquist–from the Entertainment set. © 1995 Art Parts. All rights reserved.

File name(s):
ART_19_B.WMF

Typewriter–from the Business/Travel set. © 1995 Art Parts. All rights reserved.

File name(s):
ART_20_B.WMF

File name(s):
ART_21_B.WMF

Dog–from the Animals set. © 1995 Art Parts. All rights reserved.

File name(s):
ART_22_B.WMF

Globe–from the Nature/ Environment set. © 1995 Art Parts. All rights reserved.

186

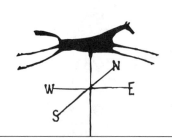

File name(s):
ART_23_B.WMF

Weather vane–from the Nature/Environment set. © 1995 Art Parts. All rights reserved.

File name(s):
ART_24_B.WMF

Swimming–from the Sports/Recreation set. © 1995 Art Parts. All rights reserved.

File name(s):
ART_25_B.WMF

Medicine–from the Faces set. © 1995 Art Parts. All rights reserved.

Chapter 9

Creative Media Services

Megatoons

Creative Media Services There are cartoons, funny cartoons, and funny-relevant cartoons.

Cartoons in general are a dime a dozen. Funny cartoons are much less common and far more valuable. Funny cartoons that are somehow relevant to your projects are rare gems. Phil Frank's Megatoons are professional quality, genuinely funny images that are designed for real applications.

Page 187: To bend over backward–from Megatoons. Below: Ladder to success–from Megatoons. © 1995 Creative Media Services. All rights reserved.

Frank has more than a little experience communicating with humor. He is the creator of *Farley,* an exclusive comic feature of the *San Francisco Chronicle* and has long been a contributing cartoonist to national publications.

With the Megatoons collections he brings his mass-market appeal to the desktop. His subject matter includes awards, business, education, events, finance, health, politics, the workplace, and others, as well as a selection of generic captioned cartoons. Each image is illustrated in Frank's signature style and charged with his trademark wit and wisdom.

Creative Media Services has been publishing Phil Frank's work since 1969. In the years since, they have syndicated his artwork (negotiated the rights to reproduce it) with thousands of corporate, campus, and healthcare publication editors who use it to bring their editorial topics to life.

188

The *Clip Art Crazy CD-ROM* includes 25 Megatoons images in a directory labeled CMS. The files are saved in the Tagged-Image File Format (TIFF) for use with both PostScript and non-PostScript printers. The file labeled READCMS.WRI (in the same directory) includes the company's license agreement, which explains when and how you can use the images, along with any other information the company elected to provide.

For more information see Appendix page 342 or contact:

Creative Media Services (CMS)

P.O. Box 5955, Berkeley, CA 94705 USA

Voice: 800-358-2278, 510-843-3408; Fax: 510-549-2490

Clothespin–from Megatoons.
© 1995 Creative Media
Services. All rights reserved.

File name(s):
CMS_01_B.TIF

Paperwork–from the Workplace category of Megatoons Part II. © 1995 Creative Media Services. All rights reserved.

File name(s):
CMS_02_B.TIF

Truck & car–from the Workplace category of Megatoons Part II. © 1995 Creative Media Services. All rights reserved.

190

File name(s):
CMS_03_B.TIF

Peace dove–from the Political category of Megatoons Part II. © 1995 Creative Media Services. All rights reserved.

File name(s):
CMS_04_B.TIF

Bicycling–from the Sports category of Megatoons Part II. © 1995 Creative Media Services. All rights reserved.

File name(s):
CMS_05_B.TIF

Handshake–from the Symbols category of Megatoons Part II. © 1995 Creative Media Services. All rights reserved.

Knife toss–from the Workplace category of Megatoons Part II. © 1995 Creative Media Services. All rights reserved.

File name(s):

CMS_06_B.TIF

Meeting–from the Captioned Cartoons category of Megatoons Part II. © 1995 Creative Media Services. All rights reserved.

File name(s):

CMS_07_B.TIF

Stress–from the Captioned Cartoons category of Megatoons. Part II. © 1995 Creative Media Services. All rights reserved.

File name(s):

CMS_08_B.TIF

191

Vacation–from the Family category of Megatoons Part II. © 1995 Creative Media Services. All rights reserved.

File name(s):

CMS_09_B.TIF

Bake sale–from the Headings category of Megatoons Part II. © 1995 Creative Media Services. All rights reserved.

File name(s):

CMS_10_B.TIF

File name(s):
CMS_11_B.TIF

Birdman–from the People category of Megatoons Part II.
© 1995 Creative Media Services. All rights reserved.

File name(s):
CMS_12_B.TIF

Sitting duck–from the Animals category of Megatoons Part II.
© 1995 Creative Media Services. All rights reserved.

192

File name(s):
CMS_13_B.TIF

Chart–from the Business category of Megatoons Part II. © 1995 Creative Media Services. All rights reserved.

File name(s):
CMS_14_B.TIF

Chef–from the Food category of Megatoons Part II. © 1995 Creative Media Services. All rights reserved.

File name(s):
CMS_15_B.TIF

Snowman–from the Seasons category of Megatoons Part II.
© 1995 Creative Media Services. All rights reserved.

Cheer–from the People category of Megatoons Part II. © 1995 Creative Media Services. All rights reserved.

File name(s):

CMS_16_B.TIF

Easter rabbit–from the Holiday category of Megatoons Part II. © 1995 Creative Media Services. All rights reserved.

File name(s):

CMS_17_B.TIF

Weight lifting–from the Health category of Megatoons Part II. © 1995 Creative Media Services. All rights reserved.

File name(s):

CMS_18_B.TIF

193

Catapult–from the Awards category of Megatoons Part II. © 1995 Creative Media Services. All rights reserved.

File name(s):

CMS_19_B.TIF

Red ink truck–from the Finance category of Megatoons Part II. © 1995 Creative Media Services. All rights reserved.

File name(s):

CMS_20_B.TIF

File name(s):
CMS_21_B.TIF

Fax man–from the Business category of Megatoons Part II.

File name(s):
CMS_22_B.TIF

Can telephone–from the Business category of Megatoons Part II.

File name(s):
CMS_23_B.TIF

Celebrate–from the Events category of Megatoons Part II.

File name(s):
CMS_24_B.TIF

Graduation–from the Education category of Megatoons Part II.

File name(s):
CMS_25_B.TIF

Memo–from the Business category of Megatoons Part II.

Chapter 10

CSA Archive Company

CSA Archive Diskette Collection & CD Sampler

CSA Archive Company Designer Charles S. Anderson has a passion for making old things new.

While some designers would be content to simply parrot a style, Anderson has invented a new one. It's a style that infuses elements of illustration and typographic design from the earlier part of this century with the knowledge and energy of a new era.

You have only to leaf through a few of the 400 plus pages of the *CSA Archive Catalog of Stock Art* to appreciate the degree of Anderson's vision. To date, Anderson and the CSA Archive Company have compiled close to 1,000,000 twentieth-century line art images. They come from every imaginable source: old books, magazines, catalogs, packaging, even cocktail napkins and matchbooks. Hundreds of others are original works by Anderson and his staff. Each illustration is selected on the merits of its content and style, and is then simplified, altered, and/or redrawn to give it the trademark CSA look.

But to appreciate the value of this collection, you need to see the mastery with which Charles S. Anderson Design Company, Anderson's much acclaimed design studio, applies the images to real projects. Projects such as the on-air identity system for the Turner Classic Movie Channel, licensed products for Paramount Pictures, or a collection of watches that is distributed through museum shops nationwide.

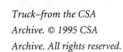

Archive clients include creative trailblazers such as Nike, Levis, MTV, and a long list of the nation's most influencial advertising agencies and design studios.

The bulk of the CSA Archive images are sold as stock cuts— you pay for the rights to use an individual image for a particular purpose. The CSA Archive CD Sampler and CSA Archive Diskette Collection are royalty-free packaged products.

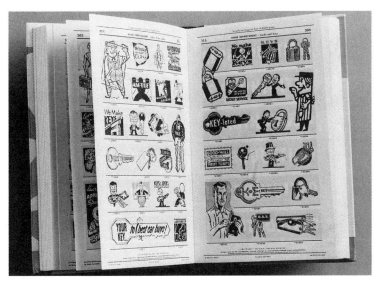

Anyone who is even remotely interested in illustration must have a copy of the CSA Archive Catalog of Stock Art. *It includes 7,777 historic and original images from the CSA Archive—the most comprehensive collection of American line art ever compiled. Crazy.*

The *Clip Art Crazy CD-ROM* includes 25 CSA Archive Diskette Collection images in a directory labeled CSA. The files are saved as PostScript (EPS). If you have a non-PostScript printer, you can import the images into a compatible drawing program and save them in a file format your software and hardware will accept, or you can invest in a conversion program that automates the process (see Use Any Image Anywhere on page 41). The file labeled READCSA.WRI (in the same directory) includes the company's license agreement, which explains when and how you can use the images, along with any other information the company elected to provide.

197

House fire–from the CSA Archive. © 1995 CSA Archive. All rights reserved.

For more information see Appendix page 345 or contact:

CSA Archive Company

P.O. Box 581639,

Minneapolis, MN 55458-1639 USA

Voice: 612-339-1263; Fax: 612-339-3283

Internet: http://www.csa-archive.com

File name(s):
CMS_01_B.EPS

Wastebasket–from the CSA Archive Diskette Collection "Split Personalities" Icons. © 1995 CSA Archive. All rights reserved.

File name(s):
CMS_02_B.EPS

Car–from the CSA Archive Diskette Collection "Route 66" Icons. © 1995 CSA Archive. All rights reserved.

198

File name(s):
CMS_03_B.EPS

Telephone–from the CSA Archive Diskette Collection "American Cheese" Illustrations. © 1995 CSA Archive. All rights reserved.

File name(s):
CMS_04_B.EPS

House fire–from the CSA Archive Diskette Collection "Wonder Bred" Illustrations. © 1995 CSA Archive. All rights reserved.

File name(s):
CMS_05_B.EPS

Turtle–from the CSA Archive Diskette Collection "Food Chain" Icons. © 1995 CSA Archive. All rights reserved.

Birthday cake–from the CSA Archive Diskette Collection "Wonder Bred" Illustrations. © 1995 CSA Archive. All rights reserved.

File name(s):

CMS_06_B.EPS

Bird–from the CSA Archive Diskette Collection "Food Chain" Icons. © 1995 CSA Archive. All rights reserved.

File name(s):

CMS_07_B.EPS

Family–from the CSA Archive Diskette Collection "Split Personalities" Icons. © 1995 CSA Archive. All rights reserved.

File name(s):

CMS_08_B.EPS

199

Indian–from the CSA Archive Diskette Collection "Daily Grind" Icons. © 1995 CSA Archive. All rights reserved.

File name(s):

CMS_09_B.EPS

Truck–from the CSA Archive Diskette Collection "Route 66" Icons. © 1995 CSA Archive. All rights reserved.

File name(s):

CMS_10_B.EPS

File name(s):
CMS_11_B.EPS

Cat–from the CSA Archive Diskette Collection "Food Chain" Icons. © 1995 CSA Archive. All rights reserved.

File name(s):
CMS_12_B.EPS

Reading–from the CSA Archive Diskette Collection "Wonder Bred" Illustrations. © 1995 CSA Archive. All rights reserved.

200

File name(s):
CMS_13_B.EPS

Bellman–from the CSA Archive Diskette Collection "Daily Grind" Icons. © 1995 CSA Archive. All rights reserved.

File name(s):
CMS_14_B.EPS

Robot–from the CSA Archive Diskette Collection "Junk Drawer" Icons. © 1995 CSA Archive. All rights reserved.

File name(s):
CMS_15_B.EPS

Running–from the CSA Archive Diskette Collection "Split Personalities" Icons. © 1995 CSA Archive. All rights reserved.

Cat–from the CSA Archive Diskette Collection "Food Chain" Icons. © 1995 CSA Archive. All rights reserved.

File name(s):
CMS_16_B.EPS

Gelatin–from the CSA Archive Diskette Collection "Junk Drawer" Icons. © 1995 CSA Archive. All rights reserved.

File name(s):
CMS_17_B.EPS

Paper–from the CSA Archive Diskette Collection "Daily Grind" Icons. © 1995 CSA Archive. All rights reserved.

File name(s):
CMS_18_B.EPS

201

Magician–from the CSA Archive Diskette Collection "American Cheese" Illustrations. © 1995 CSA Archive. All rights reserved.

File name(s):
CMS_19_B.EPS

Press proof–from the CSA Archive Diskette Collection "Split Personalities" Icons. © 1995 CSA Archive. All rights reserved.

File name(s):
CMS_20_B.EPS

File name(s):
CMS_21_B.EPS

Radiator–from the CSA Archive Diskette Collection "Junk Drawer" Icons. © 1995 CSA Archive. All rights reserved.

File name(s):
CMS_22_B.EPS

Mouse–from the CSA Archive Diskette Collection "Food Chain" Icons. © 1995 CSA Archive. All rights reserved.

File name(s):
CMS_23_B.EPS

Carpenter and toolbox–from the CSA Archive Diskette Collection "Daily Grind" Icons. © 1995 CSA Archive. All rights reserved.

File name(s):
CMS_24_B.EPS

Stress–from the CSA Archive Diskette Collection "American Cheese" Illustrations. © 1995 CSA Archive. All rights reserved.

File name(s):
CMS_25_B.EPS

Reading–from the CSA Archive Diskette Collection "Daily Grind" Icons. © 1995 CSA Archive. All rights reserved.

Chapter 11

Dynamic Graphics

Graphics Products & Services

Dynamic Graphics is king of the hill.

Established in 1964, the company actively markets its products and services worldwide through wholly owned subsidiaries in Australia, Brazil, Mexico, and the United Kingdom and through sales agents in more than 25 other countries.

Two traditional, hardcopy clip art services—Clipper and the Print Media Service—established Dynamic Graphics as a fixture in the production departments of advertising agencies, art studios, retailers, and newspapers. In recent years, electronic versions of the services—Electronic Clipper, Electronic Print Media Service, and Designer's Club (a new, exclusively electronic service)—have kept Dynamic Graphics current and relevant in a fast-changing business. Dynamic Graphics acquired and refurbished the Volk Clip Art archive in 1985 and recently added Electronic Volk as the fourth art library service.

204

Idea Source, introduced in October 1993, is the industry's first multimedia how-to magazine on CD. It uses interactive training technology to assist designers in producing creative solutions and is provided free with the CD-ROM versions of the service products. ART ON DEMAND, another service exclusive to subscribers, allows you to order specific images by mail or modem.

The newest addition is a full lineup of packaged products presented via a mail-order catalog titled *ArtWorks.* It features the Showcase Series, collections of images by notable international illustrators; the Encore Series and ArtAbout, "best of" picks from the Dynamic Graphics archives; and a PhotoConcepts Series, fonts, and other related products.

If all that isn't enough, Dynamic Graphics is also the force behind *Step-By-Step Graphics,* The How-To Magazine for

Visual Communicators; *Step-By-Step Electronic Design,* The How-To Newsletter for Electronic Designers; and the sponsor of the Dynamic Graphics Educational Foundation (DGEF), a provider of professional workshops and seminars for visual communicators.

Dynamic, it seems, is an understatement.

The *Clip Art Crazy CD-ROM* includes 25 Dynamic Graphics images in a directory labeled DYNAMIC. Some files are saved as PostScript (EPS) files for use with PostScript printers, others in the Tagged-Image File Format (TIFF) for use with both PostScript and non-PostScript printers. If you have a non-PostScript printer, you can import the EPS images into a compatible drawing program and save them in a file format your software and hardware will accept, or you can invest in a conversion program that automates the process (see Use Any Image Anywhere on page 41). The file labeled READDYN.WRI (in the same directory) includes the company's license agreement, which explains when and how you can use the images, along with any other information the company elected to provide.

For more information see Appendix page 346 or contact:

Dynamic Graphics Inc.
6000 N. Forest Park Dr.
Peoria, IL 61656-3592 USA,
Voice: 800-255-8800, 309-688-8800;
Fax: 309-688-5873
Internet: 74431.2241@compuserve.com

Office worker–from ArtWorks Ebcore Series-Business & Industry I.
© 1995 Dynamic Graphics Inc. All rights reserved.

205

File name(s):

DYN_01_B.TIF

Mother and child–from the Electronic Clipper Service. © 1995 Dynamic Graphics Inc. All rights reserved.

File name(s):

DYN_02_B.EPS

DYN_02_C.EPS

Computer–from the Designer's Club Service. © 1995 Dynamic Graphics Inc. All rights reserved.

File name(s):

DYN_03_B.EPS

Bouquet–from the Electronic Clipper Service. © 1995 Dynamic Graphics Inc. All rights reserved.

206

File name(s):

DYN_04_B.TIF

Office worker–from the Electronic Clipper Service. © 1995 Dynamic Graphics Inc. All rights reserved.

File name(s):

DYN_05_B.EPS

Scissors and comb–from the Electronic Clipper Service. © 1995 Dynamic Graphics Inc. All rights reserved.

Office workers–from the Electronic Clipper Service. © 1995 Dynamic Graphics Inc. All rights reserved.

File name(s):
DYN_06_B.TIF

Communication–from the Designer's Club Service. © 1995 Dynamic Graphics Inc. All rights reserved.

File name(s):
DYN_07_B.TIF

Breakfast–from the Designer's Club Service. © 1995 Dynamic Graphics Inc. All rights reserved.

File name(s):
DYN_08_B.EPS

207

Rain–from the Designer's Club Service. © 1995 Dynamic Graphics Inc. All rights reserved.

File name(s):
DYN_09_B.EPS

Report card–from the Designer's Club Service. © 1995 Dynamic Graphics Inc. All rights reserved.

File name(s):
DYN_10_B.EPS

File name(s):
DYN_11_B.EPS

Bird–from the Designer's Club Service © 1995 Dynamic Graphics Inc. All rights reserved.

File name(s):
DYN_12_B.TIF

Wedding ring–from the Electronic Clipper Service. © 1995 Dynamic Graphics Inc. All rights reserved.

208

File name(s):
DYN_13_B.EPS

Cricket–from the Electronic Clipper Service. © 1995 Dynamic Graphics Inc. All rights reserved.

File name(s):
DYN_14_B.EPS

Wastebasket–from the Electronic Clipper Service. © 1995 Dynamic Graphics Inc. All rights reserved.

File name(s):
DYN_15_B.TIF

Tree–from the Electronic Clipper Service. © 1995 Dynamic Graphics Inc. All rights reserved.

Barbecue–from the
Designer's Club Service.
© 1995 Dynamic
Graphics Inc. All rights
reserved.

File name(s):
DYN_16_B.EPS

Calendar of events–from
the Designer's Club
Service. © 1995
Dynamic Graphics Inc.
All rights reserved.

File name(s):
DYN_17_B.EPS

Dance–from the
Designer's Club Service.
© 1995 Dynamic
Graphics Inc. All rights
reserved.

File name(s):
DYN_18_B.EPS

209

Irish dance–from the
Electronic Clipper
Service. © 1995
Dynamic Graphics Inc.
All rights reserved.

File name(s):
DYN_19_B.EPS

Vacation–from the
Designer's Club Service.
© 1995 Dynamic
Graphics Inc. All rights
reserved.

File name(s):
DYN_20_B.EPS
DYN_20_C.EPS

File name(s):
DYN_21_B.EPS

United States Capitol–from the Designer's Club Service. © 1995 Dynamic Graphics Inc. All rights reserved.

File name(s):
DYN_22_B.EPS

Shopping cart–from the Designer's Club Service. © 1995 Dynamic Graphics Inc. All rights reserved.

File name(s):
DYN_23_B.EPS
DYN_23_C.EPS

Education–from the Designer's Club Service. © 1995 Dynamic Graphics Inc. All rights reserved.

210

File name(s):
DYN_24_B.TIF

Flowers–from the Electronic Clipper Service. © 1995 Dynamic Graphics Inc. All rights reserved.

File name(s):
DYN_25_B.EPS

Rain–from the Electronic Clipper Service. © 1995 Dynamic Graphics Inc. All rights reserved.

Chapter 12

Harter Image Archives

Harter Archive CD-ROM

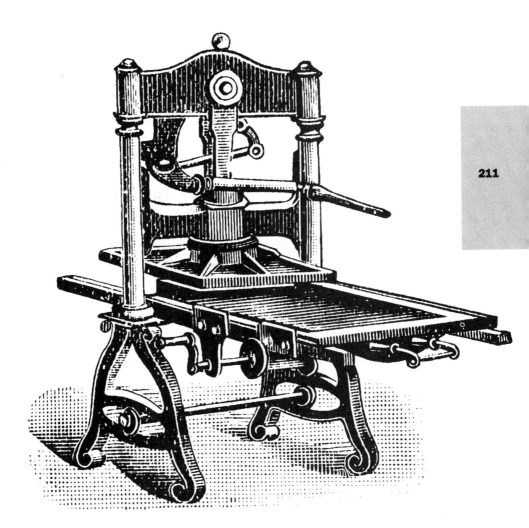

Harter Image Archives Artisans of the late 1700s perfected a technique for engraving woodblocks with beautifully intricate images of people, places, and things.

These idyllic images reflected the optimism of the time and were popular through much of the Victorian Era (a period roughly defined by the reign of England's Queen Victoria between 1837 and 1901).

Page 211: Printing press. Below: Palm tree–from Assorted Images Volume 1. © 1995 Harter Image Archives. All rights reserved.

Jim Harter first discovered this enormous body of work in a book of engraving collages, the *Cosmic Bicycle* by the late artist Sätty, and he has collected and designed with them ever since.

In 1978 Harter authored a series of books for Dover Publications featuring reprints of the images he had compiled from nineteenth century books and magazines. This popular series ended up on the bookshelves of art directors, illustrators, and connoisseurs of engravings around the world. Since 1986 Harter has produced three more works of nineteenth-century engravings for Bonanza Books on the subjects of plants, world architecture, and medicine.

The idea for Harter Image Archives was born in 1993 when another designer and computer illustrator, James Hendricks, suggested distributing antique images in electronic form. Martin Jeager joined the team as technical guru.

Together the partners have compiled a sizable library of artwork scanned and stored at between 300 dpi and 1200 dpi in the TIFF file format. There are collections of everything from books and birds to tools and toys and globes and guns. The collection is an inspired mix of elements in exquisite detail.

212

The *Clip Art Crazy CD-ROM* includes 25 Harter Archive images in a directory labeled HARTER. The files are saved in the Tagged-Image File Format (TIFF) for use with both PostScript and non-PostScript printers. The file labeled READHAR.WRI (in the same directory) includes the company's license agreement, which explains when and how you can use the images, along with any other information the company elected to provide.

For more information see Appendix page 347 or contact:

Harter Image Archives

4139 Gardendale St., #207,

San Antonio, TX 78229 USA

Voice: 210-614-5942; Fax: 210-614-5922

Book–from Assorted Images Volume 1. © 1995 Harter Image Archives. All rights reserved.

File name(s):
HAR_01_B.TIF

Bird–from Images of Men Volume 1. © 1995 Harter Image Archives. All rights reserved.

File name(s):
HAR_02_B.TIF

Punishment–from Images of Men Volume 1. © 1995 Harter Image Archives. All rights reserved.

214

File name(s):
HAR_03_B.TIF

Horse–from Images of Men Volume 1. © 1995 Harter Image Archives. All rights reserved.

File name(s):
HAR_04_B.TIF

Sled–from Assorted Images Volume 1. © 1995 Harter Image Archives. All rights reserved.

File name(s):
HAR_05_B.TIF

Music conductor–from Assorted Images Volume 1. © 1995 Harter Image Archives. All rights reserved.

*Justice–from Images of
Women Volume 1.
© 1995 Harter Image
Archives. All rights
reserved.*

File name(s):
HAR_06_B.TIF

*Cowgirl–from Images of
Women Volume 1. ©
1995 Harter Image
Archives. All rights
reserved.*

File name(s):
HAR_07_B.TIF

*Woman–from Images of
Women Volume 1.
© 1995 Harter Image
Archives. All rights
reserved.*

File name(s):
HAR_08_B.TIF

*Match–from Assorted
Images Volume 1.
© 1995 Harter Image
Archives. All rights
reserved.*

File name(s):
HAR_09_B.TIF

*Train–from Assorted
Images Volume 1.
© 1995 Harter Image
Archives. All rights
reserved.*

File name(s):
HAR_10_B.TIF

File name(s):
HAR_11_B.TIF

Shell–from Assorted Images Volume 1.

File name(s):
HAR_12_B.TIF

Palm tree–from Assorted Images Volume 1.

216

File name(s):
HAR_13_B.TIF

Rose–from Assorted Images Volume 1.

File name(s):
HAR_14_B.TIF

Cabbage–from Assorted Images Volume 1.

File name(s):
HAR_15_B.TIF

Fish–from Assorted Images Volume 1.

Aardvark–from Assorted Images Volume 1. © 1995 Harter Image Archives. All rights reserved.

File name(s):
HAR_16_B.TIF

Dragonfly–from Assorted Images Volume 1. © 1995 Harter Image Archives. All rights reserved.

File name(s):
HAR_17_B.TIF

Key–from Assorted Images Volume 1. © 1995 Harter Image Archives. All rights reserved.

File name(s):
HAR_18_B.TIF

217

Saxophone–from Assorted Images Volume 1. © 1995 Harter Image Archives. All rights reserved.

File name(s):
HAR_19_B.TIF

Printing press–from Assorted Images Volume 1. © 1995 Harter Image Archives. All rights reserved.

File name(s):
HAR_20_B.TIF

File name(s):
HAR_21_B.TIF

Book–from Assorted Images Volume 1.
© 1995 Harter Image Archives. All rights reserved.

File name(s):
HAR_22_B.TIF

Trunk–from Assorted Images Volume 1.
© 1995 Harter Image Archives. All rights reserved.

File name(s):
HAR_23_B.TIF

Dragon–from Assorted Images Volume 1.
© 1995 Harter Image Archives. All rights reserved.

218

File name(s):
HAR_24_B.TIF

Toy dog–from Assorted Images Volume 1.
© 1995 Harter Image Archives. All rights reserved.

File name(s):
HAR_25_B.TIF

Cross–from Assorted Images Volume 1.
© 1995 Harter Image Archives. All rights reserved.

Chapter 13

Iconomics
Stock & Custom Images

219

Iconomics "A forum for the purchase of design-quality illustration" is how Richard Askew, the president of Iconomics, describes the concept.

Page 21: Wine bottle and glass–by Kathy Badonsky. Below: Lightbulb by Steve Meek–from Iconomics Stock and Custom Images. © 1995 Iconomics. All rights reserved.

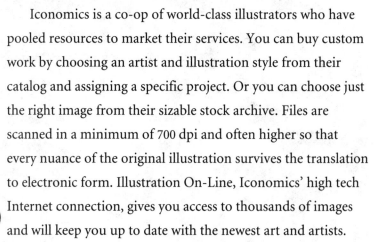

Professional illustrators typically work in two ways. You commission a custom illustration for a specific purpose and pay for the rights to use it, or you choose an image that matches your project from the "stock" of artwork they have created for other clients.

Iconomics is a co-op of world-class illustrators who have pooled resources to market their services. You can buy custom work by choosing an artist and illustration style from their catalog and assigning a specific project. Or you can choose just the right image from their sizable stock archive. Files are scanned in a minimum of 700 dpi and often higher so that every nuance of the original illustration survives the translation to electronic form. Illustration On-Line, Iconomics' high tech Internet connection, gives you access to thousands of images and will keep you up to date with the newest art and artists.

The electronic age is forcing illustrators and designers to rethink the way they do business. Superior results require a level of training and experience that does not come cheap. A forum such as this, where illustrators can meet clients and sell their wares for a reasonable return, offers the hope that the field of illustration will continue to attract new and better talent.

The *Clip Art Crazy CD-ROM* includes 25 images by Iconomic illustrators in a directory labeled ICONOMIC. The files are saved in the Tagged-Image File Format (TIFF) for use with both PostScript and non-PostScript printers. The file labeled READICN.WRI (in the same directory) includes the company's license agreement, which explains when and how you can use the images, along with any other information the company elected to provide.

Above: Town—by Brian Jensen. Below: Dinosaur by Charles Akins—from Iconomics Stock and Custom Images. © 1995 Iconomics. All rights reserved.

For more information see Appendix page 348 or contact:

Iconomics

155 N. College Ave., Fort Collins, CO 80524 USA

Voice: 800-297-7658, Fax: 303-493-6997

Internet: http://www.iconomics.com

E-mail: hipistrip@aol.com

221

File name(s):
ICN_01_B.TIF

Skull–by Alex Brown– from Iconomics Stock and Custom Images. © 1995 Iconomics. All rights reserved.

File name(s):
ICN_02_B.TIF

Telephone–by Alex Brown–from Iconomics Stock and Custom Images. © 1995 Iconomics. All rights reserved.

222

File name(s):
ICN_03_B.TIF

Town–by Brian Jensen– from Iconomics Stock and Custom Images. © 1995 Iconomics. All rights reserved.

File name(s):
ICN_04_B.TIF

Birdbath–by Brian Jensen–from Iconomics Stock and Custom Images. © 1995 Iconomics. All rights reserved.

File name(s):
ICN_05_B.TIF

Environment–by Lewis Agrell–from Iconomics Stock and Custom Images. © 1995 Iconomics. All rights reserved.

Fiddle–by Lewis Agrell–from Iconomics Stock and Custom Images. © 1995 Iconomics. All rights reserved.

File name(s):
ICN_06_B.TIF

Wine bottle and glass–by Kathy Badonsky–from Iconomics Stock and Custom Images. © 1995 Iconomics. All rights reserved.

File name(s):
ICN_07_B.TIF

Dollar bills–from stock images by Kathy Badonsky. Graphics from Iconomics Stock and Custom Images. © 1995 Iconomics. All rights reserved.

File name(s):
ICN_08_B.TIF

223

Dinosaur–by Chuck Black–from Iconomics Stock and Custom Images. © 1995 Iconomics. All rights reserved.

File name(s):
ICN_09_B.TIF

Bicycle–by Chuck Black–from Iconomics Stock and Custom Images. © 1995 Iconomics. All rights reserved.

File name(s):
ICN_10_B.TIF

File name(s):
ICN_11_B.TIF

Lightbulb–by Steve Meek–from Iconomics Stock and Custom Images. © 1995 Iconomics. All rights reserved.

File name(s):
ICN_12_B.TIF

Cigarette lighter–by Steve Meek–from Iconomics Stock and Custom Images. © 1995 Iconomics. All rights reserved.

224

File name(s):
ICN_13_B.TIF

Tomato–by Geoffrey St.James–from Iconomics Stock and Custom Images. © 1995 Iconomics. All rights reserved.

File name(s):
ICN_14_B.TIF

Pie–by Geoffrey St.James–from Iconomics Stock and Custom Images. © 1995 Iconomics. All rights reserved.

File name(s):
ICN_15_B.TIF

Insect–by Thomas Ticha–from Iconomics Stock and Custom Images. © 1995 Iconomics. All rights reserved.

Fax machine–by Peter Pohle–from Iconomics Stock and Custom Images. © 1995 Iconomics. All rights reserved.

File name(s):

ICN_16_B.TIF

Drum set–by Peter Pohle–from Iconomics Stock and Custom Images. © 1995 Iconomics. All rights reserved.

File name(s):

ICN_17_B.TIF

Meeting–by Tim Grajek–from Iconomics Stock and Custom Images. © 1995 Iconomics. All rights reserved.

File name(s):

ICN_18_B.TIF

United States Capitol– by Tim Grajek–from Iconomics Stock and Custom Images. © 1995 Iconomics. All rights reserved.

File name(s):

ICN_19_B.TIF

Office worker–by Margaret Tarleton–from Iconomics Stock and Custom Images. © 1995 Iconomics. All rights reserved.

File name(s):

ICN_20_B.TIF

File name(s):
ICN_21_B.TIF

Salesman–by Margaret Tarleton–from Iconomics Stock and Custom Images.

File name(s):
ICN_22_B.TIF

Dinosaur–by Charles Akins–from Iconomics Stock and Custom Images.

226

File name(s):
ICN_23_B.TIF

Dinosaur and cars–by Charles Akins–from Iconomics Stock and Custom Images.

File name(s):
ICN_24_B.TIF

Coffee cup–by Anne Johnstone–from Iconomics Stock and Custom Images.

File name(s):
ICN_25_B.TIF

Cows–by Anne Johnstone–from Iconomics Stock and Custom Images.

Chapter 14

Image Club Graphics

DigitArt

227

Image Club Graphics In 1987 Image Club was the first company to offer PostScript clip art.

In the years that followed, catalog marketing efforts proved so successful that Image Club was first acquired by desktop publishing pioneer Aldus, and then in 1994 by Adobe, the developer of the PostScript language, where it has been positioned as a primary marketing resource.

Today, Image Club's monthly catalog is a desktop publisher's toy store. It offers original clip art, brand name display fonts, stock photographic images, and a variety of software products. Integrated among the catalog's pages is a *Tips and Tricks Mini Magazine* that has ideas for using the images and pointers on how to create special effects. You never know what technical tidbit or new product you'll find in the next issue.

To date, Image Club has commissioned more than 36 volumes of clip art, well over 13,000 images. Among them you'll find many different styles by many different artists. Sketches on the Town-Volume 35, for example, features gestural ink sketches of food and entertainment subjects. And Silhouettes-Volume 19, is, surprisingly, one of the only collections available using this popular illustration technique.

In addition to conventional clip art images, Image Club's ever-growing PhotoGear collection of high-resolution stock photography offers business images, backgrounds, textures, scenics, fabrics, and objects.

228

Page 227: Moon–from DigitArt Fabulous Fifties-Volume 21. Above: Pottery–from DigitArt Worldbeat America-Volume 31. Right: Bicycling–from DigitArt Simple Silhouettes-Volume 19. © 1995 Image Club Graphics Inc. All rights reserved.

The *Clip Art Crazy CD-ROM* includes 25 DigitArt images in a directory labeled IMAGECLB. The files are saved as PostScript (EPS) files. If you have a non-PostScript printer, you can import the images into a compatible drawing program and save them in a file format your software and hardware will accept or you can invest in a conversion program that automates the process (see Use Any Image Anywhere on page 41). The file labeled READIMG.WRI (in the same directory) includes the company's license agreement which explains when and how you can use the images along with any other information the company elected to provide.

Skyline–from DigitArt Fabulous Fifties-Volume 21. © 1995 Image Club Graphics Inc. All rights reserved.

For more information see Appendix page 349 or contact:

Image Club Graphics Inc.

10545 West Donges Ct., Milwaukee, WI 53224-9985

Voice: 800-661-9410 (orders),

800-387-9193 (catalog requests); Fax: 403-261-7013

Internet: http://www.adobe.com/imageclub/

229

File names(s):

IMG_01_B.EPS

Piano–from Strokes and Sketches-Volume 27. © 1995 Image Club Graphics Inc. All rights reserved.

File names(s):

IMG_02_B.EPS

Photographer–from Our Environment -Volume 29. © 1995 Image Club Graphics Inc. All rights reserved.

230

File names(s):

IMG_03_B.EPS

Zebra-stripes border-Art Jam-Volume 30. © 1995 Image Club Graphics Inc. All rights reserved.

File names(s):

IMG_04_B.EPS

Taxi–from Art Jam-Volume 30. © 1995 Image Club Graphics Inc. All rights reserved.

File names(s):

IMG_05_B.EPS

Raven–from Worldbeat-Volume 31. © 1995 Image Club Graphics Inc. All rights reserved.

Bear–from Worldbeat-Volume 31. © 1995 Image Club Graphics Inc. All rights reserved.

File names(s):

IMG_06_B.EPS

Bottle–from Tom Parker's Icontents-Volume 32. © 1995 Image Club Graphics Inc. All rights reserved.

File names(s):

IMG_07_B.EPS
IMG_07_C.EPS

Magazine–from Tom Parker's Icontents-Volume 32. © 1995 Image Club Graphics Inc. All rights reserved.

File names(s):

IMG_08_B.EPS
IMG_08_C.EPS

231

Cactus–from Woodcuts-Volume 25. © 1995 Image Club Graphics Inc. All rights reserved.

File names(s):

IMG_09_B.EPS

Gardening tools–from Woodcuts-Volume 25. © 1995 Image Club Graphics Inc. All rights reserved.

File names(s):

IMG_10_B.EPS

File names(s):
IMG_11_B.EPS
IMG_11_C.EPS

Turtle–from Animals Animals-Volume 33.

File names(s):
IMG_12_B.EPS

World map–from World Maps - Volume 7.

File names(s):
IMG_13_B.EPS

Moon–from Fabulous Fifties-Volume 21.

232

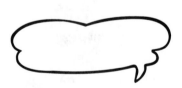

File names(s):
IMG_14_B.EPS

Talk balloon–from Fabulous Fifties-Volume 21.

File names(s):
IMG_15_B.EPS

Car–from Miscellaneous-Volume 2.

Burst–from Design Elements-Volume 9. © 1995 Image Club Graphics Inc. All rights reserved.

File names(s):
IMG_16_B.EPS

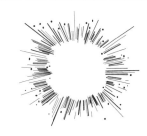

Delivery–from Business Cartoons-Volume 22. © 1995 Image Club Graphics Inc. All rights reserved.

File names(s):
IMG_17_B.EPS

Clock–from Business Cartoons-Volume 22. © 1995 Image Club Graphics Inc. All rights reserved.

File names(s):
IMG_18_B.EPS

233

Microscope–from Science & Medicine-Volume 24. © 1995 Image Club Graphics Inc. All rights reserved.

File names(s):
IMG_19_B.EPS

Blood pressure–from Science & Medicine-Volume 24. © 1995 Image Club Graphics Inc. All rights reserved.

File names(s):
IMG_20_B.EPS

File names(s):
IMG_21_B.EPS

Wreath–from Borders & Ornaments-Volume 23. © 1995 Image Club Graphics Inc. All rights reserved.

File names(s):
IMG_22_B.EPS

Cat tail–from Borders & Ornaments-Volume 23. © 1995 Image Club Graphics Inc. All rights reserved.

234

File names(s):
IMG_23_B.EPS
IMG_23_C.EPS

Horus–from Animals Animals-Volume 33. © 1995 Image Club Graphics Inc. All rights reserved.

File names(s):
IMG_24_B.EPS

Telephone–from Business Cartoons-Volume 22. © 1995 Image Club Graphics Inc. All rights reserved.

File names(s):
IMG_25_B.EPS

Banzai tree–from Borders & Ornaments-Volume 23. © 1995 Image Club Graphics Inc. All rights reserved.

Chapter 15

Letraset USA

Fontek DesignFonts

Letraset USA When you build your business on a field that is in constant flux, you must be adept at redefining yourself.

Letraset, with its innovations in typeface design, dry transfer (rub down) display fonts, graphic and drafting art tapes, color matching products, and other art studio accessories, has been a fixture of the graphic arts field for more than 30 years. But it is by no means stuck in time.

It is constantly developing new products to keep a hungry market fed. The current crop includes Fontek Digital Display and Text Fonts, a fast growing collection of classic to trendy typefaces; Paperazzi Papers, a line of high-design preprinted laser papers; the Phototone stock photo collection; and Backgrounds & Borders, a library of digital textures, patterns, and design.

236

The products featured here are tagged Fontek DesignFonts, which is a large collection of images in font form. Titles include Well Beings for health and fitness, Celebrations for a different look at holidays and special events, Journeys for travel, Mo' Funky Fresh for a collection of visual comedy, and many others. Most fonts include roughly 100 images.

DesignFonts are crafted in a variety of styles, including cut paper, pencil etching, and woodblock. Letraset has gone the extra mile to search out a world view of design, commissioning fonts from a diverse group of designers in both the United States and abroad.

The *Clip Art Crazy CD-ROM* includes 25 Fontek
DesignFont images in a directory labeled LETRASET. Though
you purchase Letraset Fontek DesignFonts as either PostScript
or TrueType fonts, the files here are individual images saved as
both PostScript (EPS) files for use with PostScript printers and
as Windows Metafiles (WMF) for use with non-PostScript
printers. The file labeled READLET.WRI (in the same directory)
includes the company's license agreement, which explains
when and how you can use the images, along with any other
information the company elected to provide.

For more information see Appendix page 349 or contact:

Letraset USA

40 Eisenhower Dr., Paramus, NJ 07653 USA

Voice: 800-343-8973, 201-845-6100; Fax: 201-845-5057

237

Globe, spiral, handshake, bottle, animal, swimming, globe, horse, eyeglasses, dog, cat, shot put–from the Primatives Fontek DesignFont. © 1995 Letraset USA. All rights reserved.

File name(s):

LET_01_B.EPS

LET_01_B.WMF

Seeing Eye dog–from the Well Beings Fontek DesignFont. © 1995 Letraset USA. All rights reserved.

File name(s):

LET_02_B.EPS

LET_02_B.WMF

Stork–from the Wildlife Fontek DesignFont. © 1995 Letraset USA. All rights reserved.

238

File name(s):

LET_03_B.EPS

LET_03_B.WMF

Shamrock–from the Organics Fontek DesignFont. © 1995 Letraset USA. All rights reserved.

File name(s):

LET_04_B.EPS

LET_04_B.WMF

Carrot-and-stick–from the Organics Fontek DesignFont. © 1995 Letraset USA. All rights reserved.

File name(s):

LET_05_B.EPS

LET_05_B.WMF

Clown–from the Primitives Fontek DesignFont. © 1995 Letraset USA. All rights reserved.

Heart–from the Radicals Fontek DesignFont. © 1995 Letraset USA. All rights reserved.	*File name(s):* LET_06_B.EPS LET_06_B.WMF	
Peppers–from the Naturals Fontek DesignFont. © 1995 Letraset USA. All rights reserved.	*File name(s):* LET_07_B.EPS LET_07_B.WMF	
Heart–from the Moderns Fontek DesignFont. © 1995 Letraset USA. All rights reserved.	*File name(s):* LET_08_B.EPS LET_08_B.WMF	
Animal–from the Mo Funky Fresh Fontek DesignFont. © 1995 Letraset USA. All rights reserved.	*File name(s):* LET_09_B.EPS LET_09_B.WMF	
Bird–from the Journeys Fontek DesignFont. © 1995 Letraset USA. All rights reserved.	*File name(s):* LET_10_B.EPS LET_10_B.WMF	

239

File name(s):
LET_11_B.EPS
LET_11_B.WMF

Umbrella–from the Incidentals Fontek DesignFont. © 1995 Letraset USA. All rights reserved.

File name(s):
LET_12_B.EPS
LET_12_B.WMF

Diver–from the Energetics Fontek DesignFont. © 1995 Letraset USA. All rights reserved.

File name(s):
LET_13_B.EPS
LET_13_B.WMF

Star–from the Inspirations Fontek DesignFont. © 1995 Letraset USA. All rights reserved.

File name(s):
LET_14_B.EPS
LET_14_B.WMF

Desk–from the Industrials Fontek DesignFont. © 1995 Letraset USA. All rights reserved.

File name(s):
LET_15_B.EPS
LET_15_B.WMF

Pottery–from the Diversions Fontek DesignFont. © 1995 Letraset USA. All rights reserved.

Rice–from the Delectables Fontek DesignFont. © 1995 Letraset USA. All rights reserved.

File name(s):
LET_16_B.EPS
LET_16_B.WMF

Television–from the Commercials Fontek DesignFont. © 1995 Letraset USA. All rights reserved.

File name(s):
LET_17_B.EPS
LET_17_B.WMF

Vacation–from the Celebrations Fontek DesignFont. © 1995 Letraset USA. All rights reserved.

File name(s):
LET_18_B.EPS
LET_18_B.WMF

241

Quill pen–from the Attitudes DesignFont. © 1995 Letraset USA. All rights reserved.

File name(s):
LET_19_B.EPS
LET_19_B.WMF

Sun–from the Calligraphic Ornaments Fontek DesignFont. © 1995 Letraset USA. All rights reserved.

File name(s):
LET_20_B.EPS
LET_20_B.WMF

File name(s):
LET_21_B.EPS
LET_21_B.WMF

Mountie–from the Custom Fontek DesignFont. © 1995 Letraset USA. All rights reserved.

File name(s):
LET_22_B.EPS
LET_22_B.WMF

Compass rose–from the Custom Fontek DesignFont. © 1995 Letraset USA. All rights reserved.

File name(s):
LET_23_B.EPS
LET_23_B.WMF

Bird–from the Custom Fontek DesignFont. © 1995 Letraset USA. All rights reserved.

242

File name(s):
LET_24_B.EPS
LET_24_B.WMF

Jumping man–from the Custom Fontek DesignFont. © 1995 Letraset USA. All rights reserved.

File name(s):
LET_25_B.EPS
LET_25_B.WMF

Rabbit–from the Custom Fontek DesignFont. © 1995 Letraset USA. All rights reserved.

Chapter 16

Metro Creative Graphics

Metro Subscription Service

Metro Creative Graphics Metro has been supplying advertisers with creative materials for 85 years, but that's the only age it shows.

Afterall, to capture and maintain a majority share of all U.S. and Canadian newspaper publishers as customers requires a keen understanding of consumer markets and trends, and a willingness to change.

Customers use Metro's illustration and editorial subscription services primarily to compose advertisements, advertising sections in newspapers, and business publications. But the subject matter, quality, and price of their artwork is worth a look by any desktop publisher.

Their services include the Metro Newspaper Service, a monthly collection of original artwork and ideas for holidays, special events, and general advertising; Classified Dynamics, for creating recruitment, automotive, real estate, and other theme classified sections, an annual Holiday Advertising Service, with images and ideas for promoting the Christmas holiday season; and Special Sections, for creating gardening, bridal, holiday, and other theme editorial supplements.

Sales Spectaculars, a preview of things to come, is a collection of ready-to-use ads for retailers in the form of desktop publishing files. You add your information and print the results.

All of the services are available in digital form on Metro's LaserArt CD-ROM as EPS or TIFF files or in traditional print form. Plus Business, a monthly compendium of marketing and advertising ideas, is included with most subscription packages.

In large part, the only folks who know about and use Metro's products and services are newspaper publishers and a handful of their advertisers. Now you, too, know where to find

Newspapers–from Metro Subscription Service. © 1995 Metro Creative Graphics Inc. All rights reserved.

this premier collection of art elements, tools, and ideas.

The *Clip Art Crazy CD-ROM* includes 25 Metro Creative Graphics images in a directory labeled METRO. Some files are saved as PostScript (EPS) files for use with PostScript printers, others in the Tagged-Image File Format (TIFF) for use with both PostScript and non-PostScript printers. If you have a non-PostScript printer, you can import the EPS images into a compatible drawing program and save them in a file format your software and hardware will accept, or you can invest in a conversion program that automates the process (see Use Any Image Anywhere on page 41). The file labeled READMET.WRI (in the same directory) includes the company's license agreement, which explains when and how you can use the images, along with any other information the company elected to provide.

Page 243: Award ribbon– from Metro Subscription Service. Opposite: To hang by a thread–from Metro Subscription Service. © 1995 Metro Creative Graphics Inc. All rights reserved.

For more information see Appendix page 351 or contact:

Metro Creative Graphics Inc.

33 West 34th St., New York, NY 10001 USA

Voice: 800-223-1600, 212-947-5100, Fax: 212-967-4602

245

File format(s):
MET_01_B.EPS

Surgeon–from Metro Subscription Service.

File format(s):
MET_02_B.TIF

Dog–from Metro Subscription Service.

246

File format(s):
MET_03_B.TIF

Scientist–from Metro Subscription Service.

File format(s):
MET_04_B.TIF

Grapes–from Metro Subscription Service.

File format(s):
MET_05_B.TIF

Mailbox–from Metro Subscription Service.

Pretzel–from Metro Subscription Service. © 1995 Metro Creative Graphics Inc. All rights reserved.

File format(s):
MET_06_B.TIF

Mexican food–from Metro Subscription Service. © 1995 Metro Creative Graphics Inc. All rights reserved.

File format(s):
MET_07_B.TIF

Guitar, trumpet, drum– from Metro Subscription Service. © 1995 Metro Creative Graphics Inc. All rights reserved.

File format(s):
MET_08_B.TIF

247

Sandwich–from Metro Subscription Service. © 1995 Metro Creative Graphics Inc. All rights reserved.

File format(s):
MET_09_B.TIF

Observatory–from Metro Subscription Service. © 1995 Metro Creative Graphics Inc. All rights reserved.

File format(s):
MET_10_B.TIF

File format(s):
MET_11_B.TIF

Tennis–from Metro Subscription Service. © 1995 Metro Creative Graphics Inc. All rights reserved.

File format(s):
MET_12_B.EPS

Place setting–from Metro Subscription Service. © 1995 Metro Creative Graphics Inc. All rights reserved.

File format(s):
MET_13_B.TIF

Cello–from Metro Subscription Service. © 1995 Metro Creative Graphics Inc. All rights reserved.

248

File format(s):
MET_14_B.EPS

Cappuccino maker–from Metro Subscription Service. © 1995 Metro Creative Graphics Inc. All rights reserved.

File format(s):
MET_15_B.EPS

Cowboy–from Metro Subscription Service. © 1995 Metro Creative Graphics Inc. All rights reserved.

Genie–from Metro Subscription Service. © 1995 Metro Creative Graphics Inc. All rights reserved.

File format(s):
MET_16_B.EPS

Popcorn–from Metro Subscription Service. © 1995 Metro Creative Graphics Inc. All rights reserved.

File format(s):
MET_17_B.EPS

Golf–from Metro Subscription Service. © 1995 Metro Creative Graphics Inc. All rights reserved.

File format(s):
MET_18_B.EPS

249

Money–from Metro Subscription Service. © 1995 Metro Creative Graphics Inc. All rights reserved.

File format(s):
MET_19_B.TIF

Cold–from Metro Subscription Service. © 1995 Metro Creative Graphics Inc. All rights reserved.

File format(s):
MET_20_B.EPS

File format(s):
MET_21_B.TIF

Sailboat–from Metro Subscription Service. © 1995 Metro Creative Graphics Inc. All rights reserved.

File format(s):
MET_22_B.TIF

Newspapers–from Metro Subscription Service. © 1995 Metro Creative Graphics Inc. All rights reserved.

File format(s):
MET_23_B.TIF

To hang by a thread– from Metro Subscription Service. © 1995 Metro Creative Graphics Inc. All rights reserved.

250

File format(s):
MET_24_B.TIF

Friends–from Metro Subscription Service. © 1995 Metro Creative Graphics Inc. All rights reserved.

File format(s):
MET_25_B.TIF

Award ribbon–from Metro Subscription Service. © 1995 Metro Creative Graphics Inc. All rights reserved.

Chapter 17

MvB Design

MvB Image Fonts & MvB Archive

MvB Design Mark van Bronkhorst is fluent in many dialects of the visual language.

With his PictureFont series for FontHaus, he captures the idyllic, crafted style of the 1920s and 30s. With Celestia Ornaments he reveals a loose, lyrical side. And with his quirky Dick & Jane font series he demonstrates a knack for saying new things in new ways. In both his illustrations and type designs (Magnesium, Celestia Antiqua, and others) he demonstrates a deft talent for reducing complex ideas to simple expressions.

But MvB Design is not a one-man show. Mark van Bronkhorst is surrounded by Kanna Aoki, the designer of Greymantle and Emmascript fonts; Akemi Aoki, creator of the Acme font series; and Georgia Panagiotopoulos, the hand behind DogHaus, Canyonlands, Horny Dave, and others. Together they are creating and compiling some significant collections of out-of-the-ordinary art: retro ad cuts from the 1920s through the 50s, a revival of nineteenth-century printer's cuts, offbeat creations by other designers, among others.

When they are not producing products, van Bronkhorst and company are designing type and images for clients, includ-

Cowboy–from Dick & Jane font by Mark van Bronkhorst.

Pixie–from Horny Dave font by Georgia Panagiotopoulos.

Skyline–from the FontHaus PictureFonts Commerce & Communication.

Crocodile–from The Return of Dick & Jane font by Mark van Bronkhorst.

ing a major motion picture company, a children's book publisher, a software manufacturer, and a few national magazines.

The *Clip Art Crazy* CD-ROM includes 25 MvB samples in a

directory labeled MVB. Though you purchase some of the MvB products as either PostScript or TrueType fonts, the files here are individual images saved as both PostScript (EPS) files for use with PostScript printers and as Windows Metafiles (WMF) for use with non-PostScript printers. The file labeled READMVB.WRI (in the same directory) includes the company's license agreement, which explains when and how you can use the images, along with any other information the company elected to provide.

Cars and recreational vehicle–from The Return of Dick & Jane font by Mark van Bronkhorst.

For more information see Appendix page 351 or contact:
MvB Design
Available from FontHaus Inc.,
1375 Kings Hwy. East, Fairfield, CT 06430 USA
Voice: 800-942-9110, 203-367-1993; Fax: 203-367-1860

253

Images on this page–from MvB fonts and MvB Archive. © 1995 MvB Design. All rights reserved.

Teeth–from the FontHaus PictureFonts Household Items.

Firecrackers–from the FontHaus PictureFonts Holidays & Celebrations.

Apples–from the AcmeGreenGarden font by Akemi Aoki.

Seaplane–from the FontHaus PictureFonts Transportation & Travel.

File name(s):
MVB_01_B.WMF

Pyramid–from the FontHaus PictureFonts Transportation & Travel (product in font format). © 1995 MvB Design. All rights reserved.

File name(s):
MVB_02_B.WMF

Ship–from the FontHaus PictureFonts Transportation & Travel (product in font format). © 1995 MvB Design. All rights reserved.

254

File name(s):
MVB_03_B.WMF

Pointing hand–from the FontHaus PictureFonts Commerce & Communication (product in font format). © 1995 MvB Design. All rights reserved.

File name(s):
MVB_04_B.WMF

Delivery scooter–from the FontHaus PictureFonts Commerce & Communication (product in font format). © 1995 MvB Design. All rights reserved.

File name(s):
MVB_05_B.WMF

Gingerbread man–from the FontHaus PictureFonts Holidays & Celebrations (product in font format). © 1995 MvB Design. All rights reserved.

Candy heart–from the FontHaus PictureFonts Holidays & Celebrations (product in font format). © 1995 MvB Design. All rights reserved.

File name(s):
MVB_06_B.WMF

Hot dog–from the FontHaus PictureFonts Food & Drink (product in font format). © 1995 MvB Design. All rights reserved.

File name(s):
MVB_07_B.WMF

Electricity–from AcmeServices by Akemi Aoki (product in font format). © 1995 MvB Design. All rights reserved.

File name(s):
MVB_08_B.WMF

255

Lightbulb–from the FontHaus PictureFonts Household Items (product in font format). © 1995 MvB Design. All rights reserved.

File name(s):
MVB_09_B.WMF

Chicken–from the FontHaus PictureFonts Animals (product in font format). © 1995 MvB Design. All rights reserved.

File name(s):
MVB_10_B.WMF

File name(s):
MVB_11_B.WMF

Sailor–from Dick & Jane by Mark van Bronkhorst (product in font format). © 1995 MvB Design. All rights reserved.

File name(s):
MVB_12_B.WMF

Bird in roller skate–from Dick & Jane by Mark van Bronkhorst (product in font format). © 1995 MvB Design. All rights reserved.

File name(s):
MVB_13_B.WMF

Skeletons in the closet– from The Return of Dick & Jane by Mark van Bronkhorst (product in font format). © 1995 MvB Design. All rights reserved.

File name(s):
MVB_14_B.WMF

Coffee cup–from AcmeWhatever by Akemi Aoki (product in font format). © 1995 MvB Design. All rights reserved.

File name(s):
MVB_15_B.WMF

Fish–from AcmeAnimals by Akemi Aoki (product in font format). © 1995 MvB Design. All rights reserved.

Dinosaur–from AcmeDinosaurs by Akemi Aoki (product in font format). © 1995 MvB Design. All rights reserved.

File name(s):

MVB_16_B.WMF

Whistle–from AcmeSports'nGames by Akemi Aoki (product in font format). © 1995 MvB Design. All rights reserved.

File name(s):

MVB_17_B.WMF

Deer–from MvB Archive Canonlands by Georgia Panagiotopoulos (product in EPS/WMF formats). © 1995 MvB Design. All rights reserved.

File name(s):

MVB_18_B.WMF

257

Skunk–from MvB Archive Zoology 101 by Georgia Panagiotopoulos (product in EPS/WMF formats). © 1995 MvB Design. All rights reserved.

File name(s):

MVB_19_B.WMF

Angel–from Celestia Ornaments (font of ornaments to complement Celestia typeface family by MvB). © 1995 MvB Design. All rights reserved.

File name(s):

MVB_20_B.WMF

File name(s):
MVB_21_B.WMF

Dog–from MvB Archive Scratch 'n Sniff by Georgia Panagiotopoulos (product in EPS/WMF formats). © 1995 MvB Design. All rights reserved.

File name(s):
MVB_22_B.WMF

Dog–from MvB Archive DogHaus by Georgia Panagiotopoulos (product in EPS/WMF formats). © 1995 MvB Design. All rights reserved.

258

File name(s):
MVB_23_B.WMF

Pixie–from Horny Dave by Georgia Panagiotopoulos (product in font format). © 1995 MvB Design. All rights reserved.

File name(s):
MVB_24_B.WMF

Grasshopper–from AcmeGreenGarden by Akemi Aoki (product in font format). © 1995 MvB Design. All rights reserved.

File name(s):
MVB_25_B.WMF

Cat and kittens–from MvB Archive CatHaus by Georgia Panagiotopoulos (product in EPS/WMF formats). © 1995 MvB Design. All rights reserved.

Chapter 18

New Vision Technologies

Presentation & Publisher's Task Force

New Vision Technologies Graphics for the real world.

Peter Heney and his crew at New Vision Technologies have created a collection of high-quality graphics that can be used with just about any hardware and software configuration you can imagine. To do it they chose the two file formats that work with the widest range of programs: Computer Graphics Metafiles (CGM), a vector graphics standard for software used under the DOS operating system; and Windows Metafiles (WMF), a vector graphics standard for programs that operate within Windows. Both are formats that print at their best without a PostScript printer and that require a fraction of the space needed by a typical bitmapped file.

Page 259: Electricity–from Publisher's Task Force. Below: Pole-vault–from Publisher's Task Force. © 1995 New Vision Technologies Inc. All rights reserved.

Next, they developed a drawing style that takes best advantage of those formats—a clean, chiseled look that easily accommodates both color and grayscales, and that approximates the kinds of fills and gradations that typically require a PostScript printer.

Finally (for Windows users), they packaged the files within a slick utility—Task Force Commander—which allows you to search for and view images, change color and grayscale palettes, save the files as black-and-white line art, change the images to silhouettes, and more.

260

But don't think for a minute that a first-class technical approach means second-class graphics. The New Vision style is distinctive enough to grab attention without being overbearing. In addition to the standard categories such as people, sports, and industry, these wide-ranging collections include some unusual but useful topics such as architecture, transportation, military, medical, and a polished collection of cartoons.

The *Clip Art Crazy CD-ROM* includes 25 Presentation Task Force and Publisher's Task Force images in a directory labeled NWVISION. The files are saved as both Computer Graphics Metafiles (CGM) files for use with DOS programs and as Windows Metafiles (WMF) for use with Windows programs. Both file formats can be printed on PostScript and non-PostScript printers. The file labeled READNEW.WRI (in the same directory) includes the company's license agreement, which explains when and how you can use the images, along with any other information the company elected to provide.

For more information see Appendix page 353 or contact:

New Vision Technologies Inc.
38 Auriga Drive, Unit 13,
Nepean, Ontario, Canada K2E 8A5
Voice: 800-387-0732, 613-727-8184;
Fax: 613-727-8190

Large and small views of the watch illustration show how CGM and WMF files can be enlarged or reduced with no loss of detail.

261

File name(s):
NEW_01_C.CGM
NEW_01_C.WMF

Fish–from the World of Animals category of Presentation Task Force. © 1995 New Vision Technologies Inc. All rights reserved.

File name(s):
NEW_02_C.CGM
NEW_02_C.WMF

Pot of gold–from the World of Business & Finance category of Presentation Task Force. © 1995 New Vision Technologies Inc. All rights reserved.

262

File name(s):
NEW_03_C.CGM
NEW_03_C.WMF

Bicycling–from the Cartoons category of Presentation Task Force. © 1995 New Vision Technologies Inc. All rights reserved.

File name(s):
NEW_04_C.CGM
NEW_04_C.WMF

Stopwatch–from the Expressive Hands category of Presentation Task Force. © 1995 New Vision Technologies Inc. All rights reserved.

File name(s):
NEW_05_C.CGM
NEW_05_C.WMF

Bird–from the Animals category of Publisher's Task Force-Volume 1. © 1995 New Vision Technologies Inc. All rights reserved.

Electricity–from the Cartoons category of Publisher's Task Force-Volume 1. © 1995 New Vision Technologies Inc. All rights reserved.

File name(s):

NEW_06_C.CGM

NEW_06_C.WMF

Ship–from the Transportation category of Publisher's Task Force-Volume 1. © 1995 New Vision Technologies Inc. All rights reserved.

File name(s):

NEW_07_C.CGM

NEW_07_C.WMF

Broccoli–from the Cartoons category of Publisher's Task Force-Volume 1. © 1995 New Vision Technologies Inc. All rights reserved.

File name(s):

NEW_08_C.CGM

NEW_08_C.WMF

263

Director's chair–from the Miscellaneous Objects category of Publisher's Task Force-Volume 1. © 1995 New Vision Technologies Inc. All rights reserved.

File name(s):

NEW_09_C.CGM

NEW_09_C.WMF

Sextant–from the Miscellaneous Objects category of Publisher's Task Force-Volume 1. © 1995 New Vision Technologies Inc. All rights reserved.

File name(s):

NEW_10_C.CGM

NEW_10_C.WMF

File name(s):

NEW_11_C.CGM

NEW_11_C.WMF

Japanese castle–from the Architecture category of Publisher's Task Force-Volume 1. © 1995 New Vision Technologies Inc. All rights reserved.

File name(s):

NEW_12_C.CGM

NEW_12_C.WMF

Accordion–from the Music category of Publisher's Task Force-Volume 1. © 1995 New Vision Technologies Inc. All rights reserved.

264

File name(s):

NEW_13_C.CGM

NEW_13_C.WMF

Ladybug–from the Symbols category of Publisher's Task Force-Volume 1. © 1995 New Vision Technologies Inc. All rights reserved.

File name(s):

NEW_14_C.CGM

NEW_14_C.WMF

Shark-infested waters– from the Cartoons category of Presentation Task Force. © 1995 New Vision Technologies Inc. All rights reserved.

File name(s):

NEW_15_C.CGM

NEW_15_C.WMF

Glue, tape, scissors–from the World of Business & Finance category of Presentation Task Force. © 1995 New Vision Technologies Inc. All rights reserved.

Helicopter–from the World of Transportation category of Presentation Task Force. © 1995 New Vision Technologies Inc. All rights reserved.

File name(s):

NEW_16_C.CGM

NEW_16_C.WMF

F15 jet–from the World of Defense category of Presentation Task Force. © 1995 New Vision Technologies Inc. All rights reserved.

File name(s):

NEW_17_C.CGM

NEW_17_C.WMF

Father and child–from the People category of Publisher's Task Force-Volume 1. © 1995 New Vision Technologies Inc. All rights reserved.

File name(s):

NEW_18_C.CGM

NEW_18_C.WMF

265

Juggler–from the People category of Publisher's Task Force-Volume 1. © 1995 New Vision Technologies Inc. All rights reserved.

File name(s):

NEW_19_C.CGM

NEW_19_C.WMF

Building–from the Fonts & Dingbats category of Publisher's Task Force-Volume 1. © 1995 New Vision Technologies Inc. All rights reserved.

File name(s):

NEW_20_C.CGM

NEW_20_C.WMF

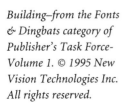

File name(s):
NEW_21_C.CGM
NEW_21_C.WMF

Keys–from the World of Transportation category of Presentation Task Force. © 1995 New Vision Technologies Inc. All rights reserved.

File name(s):
NEW_22_C.CGM
NEW_22_C.WMF

Traffic signal–from the World of Transportation category of Presentation Task Force. © 1995 New Vision Technologies Inc. All rights reserved.

File name(s):
NEW_23_C.CGM
NEW_23_C.WMF

Arrow–from the Arrows & Text Enhancers category of Presentation Task Force. © 1995 New Vision Technologies Inc. All rights reserved.

File name(s):
NEW_24_C.CGM
NEW_24_C.WMF

Backhoe–from the Transportation category of Publisher's Task Force-Volume 1. © 1995 New Vision Technologies Inc. All rights reserved.

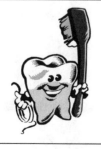

File name(s):
NEW_25_C.CGM
NEW_25_C.WMF

Toothbrush–from the Cartoons category of Presentation Task Force. © 1995 New Vision Technologies Inc. All rights reserved.

Chapter 19

The Oswego Company

Oswego Illustrated Archives

Stainless
Steel

The Oswego Company Look closely—these are not photographs. They are PostScript images created in Adobe Illustrator by a world leader in digital graphics.

When you see the full Oswego Illustrated Archives, you'll be astounded at what it includes. For about what it would cost to hire a proficient artist for a couple of hours of custom

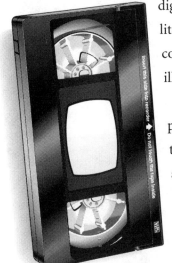

digitizing, you can buy a body of images that represents literally thousands of hours of work. Pixel by pixel, this collection contains some of the most precise, realistic illustration you will find.

The Oswego Company has been generating photorealistic illustrations for prominent international corporations and leading advertising agencies since 1986. The archive includes some of the company's "greatest hits," minus the trade names and identifying markings. The advantages are obvious—you can use the images as is or you can edit them for use in layouts, comps, or within actual collateral, signage, or packaging. Because they are in EPS vector form, you can reduce or enlarge them to any size without compromising their exceptional detail.

Above all, the archive is a portfolio of work that demonstrates the skills of a talented group of people. The Oswego Company has the facilities to re-create and output all kinds of custom illustrations in both color and black and white. If you have objects or ideas that you need in computer form, these are the folks to create it.

Page 267: Coffee pot–from the Home Appliances category. Above: Videotape–from the Home Electronics category of the Oswego Illustrated Archives. © 1995 Oswego Company. All rights reserved.

268

The *Clip Art Crazy CD-ROM* includes 25 images from the Oswego Illustrated Archives in a directory labeled OSWEGO. The files are saved as PostScript (EPS) files. If you have a non-PostScript printer, you can import the images into a compatible drawing program and save them in a file format your software and hardware will accept or you can invest in a conversion program that automates the process (see Use Any Image Anywhere on page 41). The file labeled READOSW.WRI (in the same directory) includes the company's license agreement, which explains when and how you can use the images, along with any other information the company elected to provide.

For more information see Appendix page 354 or contact:

The Oswego Company

610 SW Alder St. #609,

Portland, OR 97205 USA

Voice: 800-275-1989, 503-274-9338; Fax: 503-274-9326

Car–from the Transportation & Travel category of the Oswego Illustrated Archives.

269

File name(s):
OSW_01_B.EPS

Chandelier–from the Architecture category of the Oswego Illustrated Archives. © 1995 Oswego Company. All rights reserved.

File name(s):
OSW_02_B.EPS

Calculator–from the Business category of the Oswego Illustrated Archives. © 1995 Oswego Company. All rights reserved.

File name(s):
OSW_03_B.EPS

File cabinets–from the Business category of the Oswego Illustrated Archives. © 1995 Oswego Company. All rights reserved.

File name(s):
OSW_04_B.EPS

Pencils–from the Business category of the Oswego Illustrated Archives. © 1995 Oswego Company. All rights reserved.

File name(s):
OSW_05_C.EPS

Lilies–from the Flora & Fauna category of the Oswego Illustrated Archives. © 1995 Oswego Company. All rights reserved.

Beer–from the Food category of the Oswego Illustrated Archives. © 1995 Oswego Company. All rights reserved.

File name(s):

OSW_06_B.EPS

Faucet–from the Hardware category of the Oswego Illustrated Archives. © 1995 Oswego Company. All rights reserved.

File name(s):

OSW_07_B.EPS

Refrigerator–from the Home Appliances category of the Oswego Illustrated Archives. © 1995 Oswego Company. All rights reserved.

File name(s):

OSW_08_B.EPS

271

Coffee pot–from the Home Appliances category of the Oswego Illustrated Archives. © 1995 Oswego Company. All rights reserved.

File name(s):

OSW_09_B.EPS

Radio–from the Home Electronics category of the Oswego Illustrated Archives. © 1995 Oswego Company. All rights reserved.

File name(s):

OSW_10_B.EPS

File name(s):

OSW_11_B.EPS

Computer–from the Home Electronics category of the Oswego Illustrated Archives.

File name(s):

OSW_12_B.EPS

Cellular telephone–from the Home Electronics category of the Oswego Illustrated Archives.

272

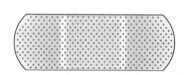

File name(s):

OSW_13_B.EPS

Videotape–from the Home Electronics category of the Oswego Illustrated Archives.

File name(s):

OSW_14_C.EPS

Bandage–from the Miscellaneous category of the Oswego Illustrated Archives.

File name(s):

OSW_15_B.EPS

ATM machine–from the Miscellaneous category of the Oswego Illustrated Archives.

Car radio–from the
Mobile Electronics
category of the Oswego
Illustrated Archives.
© 1995 Oswego
Company. All rights
reserved.

File name(s):
OSW_16_B.EPS

Piano–from the
Musical Instruments
category of the Oswego
Illustrated Archives.
© 1995 Oswego
Company. All rights
reserved.

File name(s):
OSW_17_B.EPS

Golf club–from the
Sports category of the
Oswego Illustrated
Archives. © 1995
Oswego Company. All
rights reserved.

File name(s):
OSW_18_B.EPS

273

Baseball glove–from the
Sports category of the
Oswego Illustrated
Archives. © 1995
Oswego Company. All
rights reserved.

File name(s):
OSW_19_B.EPS

Fishing lure–from the
Sports category of the
Oswego Illustrated
Archives. © 1995
Oswego Company. All
rights reserved.

File name(s):
OSW_20_B.EPS

File name(s):

OSW_21_B.EPS

Tennis racquet-From
the Sports category of
the Oswego Illustrated
Archives. © 1995
Oswego Company. All
rights reserved.

File name(s):

OSW_22_B.EPS

Motorcycle–from the
Transportation &
Travel category of the
Oswego Illustrated
Archives. © 1995
Oswego Company. All
rights reserved.

274

File name(s):

OSW_23_B.EPS

Bicycle–from the
Transportation &
Travel category of the
Oswego Illustrated
Archives. © 1995
Oswego Company. All
rights reserved.

File name(s):

OSW_24_B.EPS

Car–from the
Transportation &
Travel category of the
Oswego Illustrated
Archives. © 1995
Oswego Company. All
rights reserved.

File name(s):

OSW_25_B.EPS

Airliner–from the
Transportation &
Travel category of the
Oswego Illustrated
Archives. © 1995
Oswego Company. All
rights reserved.

Chapter 20
Daniel Pelavin
Daniel Pelavin's Illustrated Stock Cuts

Daniel Pelavin You build a career in design and illustration by honing your skills, first on fictitious projects dreamed up by instructors, then by working on real projects for people who have no money, and finally (if you survive) you graduate to working for real clients with real budgets.

Along the way, you join and contribute to professional organizations and submit your work to publications and competitions in order to build your reputation among the clients and colleagues who buy your services. It is no piece of cake. The only thing that could possibly make it more difficult would be to attempt it in the design capital of the world—New York City.

Daniel Pelavin has paid his dues. His spot illustrations and the precisely drafted shapes, unique color palette, and original typography of his design work have earned him international recognition. Along the way he has been recognized by the American Institute of Graphic Arts, the Society of Illustrators, the Type Director's Club, *Graphis*, *Print*, and *Communication Arts*, and other organiza tions and publications too numerous to mention.

Daniel Pelavin's *Illustrated Stock Cuts for Art Directors* is an archive catalog of over 1,000 of his spot illustrations, now in its third edition. Designers and art directors for advertising agencies, art studios, and publishers around the world have been using

276

Pelavin's stock illustrations and commissioning custom work for 25 years.

In the past, Pelavin has sold the images as stock cuts only—you pay for the rights to use individual images for a particular purpose. But now, for the first time, he is offering a limited collection of packaged images.

The *Clip Art Crazy CD-ROM* includes 25 of Pelavin's *Illustrated Stock Cuts* in a directory labeled PELAVIN, a preview of the collection. The files are saved as PostScript (EPS) files. If you have a non-PostScript printer, you can import the images into a compatible drawing program and save them in a file format your software and hardware will accept, or you can invest in a conversion program that automates the process (see Use Any Image Anywhere on page 41). The file labeled READPEL.WRI (in the same directory) includes the company's license agreement, which explains when and how you can use the images, along with any other information the company elected to provide.

For more information see Appendix page 353 or contact:
Daniel Pelavin
80 Varick St. #3B, New York, NY 10013 USA
Voice: 212-941-7418, Fax: 212-431-7138
Internet: dpelavin@inch.com

Reading–from Illustrated Stock Cuts. © 1995 Daniel Pelavin. All rights reserved.

277

File name(s):
PEL_01_B.EPS

Rocket–from the Transportation category of Illustrated Stock Cuts. © 1995 Daniel Pelavin. All rights reserved.

File name(s):
PEL_02_B.EPS

Horse racing–from the Animals category of Illustrated Stock Cuts. © 1995 Daniel Pelavin. All rights reserved.

278

File name(s):
PEL_03_B.EPS

Dog–from the Animals category of Illustrated Stock Cuts. © 1995 Daniel Pelavin. All rights reserved.

File name(s):
PEL_04_B.EPS

Radio–from the Arts & Entertainment category of Illustrated Stock Cuts. © 1995 Daniel Pelavin. All rights reserved.

File name(s):
PEL_05_B.EPS

Bomb–from the Tools & Machinery category of Illustrated Stock Cuts. © 1995 Daniel Pelavin. All rights reserved.

Thread and buttons–
from the Household
category of Illustrated
Stock Cuts. © *1995*
Daniel Pelavin. All
rights reserved.

File name(s):
PEL_06_B.EPS

Truck–from the
Transportation category
of Illustrated Stock Cuts.
© *1995 Daniel Pelavin.*
All rights reserved.

File name(s):
PEL_07_B.EPS

Church–from the
Buildings category of
Illustrated Stock Cuts.
© *1995 Daniel Pelavin.*
All rights reserved.

File name(s):
PEL_08_B.EPS

279

House–from the
Buildings category of
Illustrated Stock Cuts.
© *1995 Daniel Pelavin.*
All rights reserved.

File name(s):
PEL_09_B.EPS

Tractor–from the
Transportation category
of Illustrated Stock Cuts.
© *1995 Daniel Pelavin.*
All rights reserved.

File name(s):
PEL_10_B.EPS

File name(s):
PEL_11_B.EPS

Exercise bicycle–from the Health & Medicine category of Illustrated Stock Cuts. © 1995 Daniel Pelavin. All rights reserved.

File name(s):
PEL_12_B.EPS

Doctor–from the People category of Illustrated Stock Cuts. © 1995 Daniel Pelavin. All rights reserved.

File name(s):
PEL_13_B.EPS

Blood pressure–from the Health & Medicine category of Illustrated Stock Cuts. © 1995 Daniel Pelavin. All rights reserved.

280

File name(s):
PEL_14_B.EPS

Listen–from the Sports category of Illustrated Stock Cuts. © 1995 Daniel Pelavin. All rights reserved.

File name(s):
PEL_15_B.EPS

Mail–from the Business & Communications category of Illustrated Stock Cuts. © 1995 Daniel Pelavin. All rights reserved.

Street sign–from the Decorative & Symbols category of Illustrated Stock Cuts. © 1995 Daniel Pelavin. All rights reserved.

File name(s):
PEL_16_B.EPS

Factory–from the Buildings category of Illustrated Stock Cuts. © 1995 Daniel Pelavin. All rights reserved.

File name(s):
PEL_17_B.EPS

Reading–from the People category of Illustrated Stock Cuts. © 1995 Daniel Pelavin. All rights reserved.

File name(s):
PEL_18_B.EPS

281

Airliner–from the Transportation category of Illustrated Stock Cuts. © 1995 Daniel Pelavin. All rights reserved.

File name(s):
PEL_19_B.EPS

Telescope–from the Environment category of Illustrated Stock Cuts. © 1995 Daniel Pelavin. All rights reserved.

File name(s):
PEL_20_B.EPS

File name(s):
PEL_21_B.EPS

Ice cream bar–from the Food & Dining category of Illustrated Stock Cuts. © 1995 Daniel Pelavin. All rights reserved.

File name(s):
PEL_22_B.EPS

Suitcase–from the Travel category of Illustrated Stock Cuts. © 1995 Daniel Pelavin. All rights reserved.

282

File name(s):
PEL_23_B.EPS

Computer keyboard from the Business & Communications category of Illustrated Stock Cuts. © 1995 Daniel Pelavin. All rights reserved.

File name(s):
PEL_24_B.EPS

Circuit board with houses–from the Tools & Machinery category of Illustrated Stock Cuts. © 1995 Daniel Pelavin. All rights reserved.

File name(s):
PEL_25_B.EPS

Place setting–from the Food & Dining category of Illustrated Stock Cuts. © 1995 Daniel Pelavin. All rights reserved.

Chapter 21

Periwinkle Software

Past-Tints

Periwinkle Software Carol Stickley has a wonderful eye for antique illustrations.

Though there have been many hundreds of thousands of illustrations created since the advent of the printing press, there are a finite number that have the personality of the ones Stickley has compiled.

You don't come by art of this caliber easily. As a graphic designer, Carol began collecting and cataloging illustrations years ago, to use in projects for her clients. But it wasn't until the exploding popularity of CD-ROM storage that publishing the collection became practical.

Since 1994 Stickley has published a number of titles with the help of sons Jonathan and Daniel. Among them are the Past-Tints Sampler Edition featuring tidbits from a variety of categories; the Garden Edition with images from the outdoors, such as flowers, vegetables, fruits, and birds; the Home Edition with holidays, food, romance, and household inventions; and the Transportation Edition, which includes automobiles, trains, aircraft, and ships.

Page 283: Lilies–from the Past-Tints Sampler Edition. Right: Biplane– from the Past-Tints Sampler Edition. © 1995 Periwinkle Software. All rights reserved.

To retain as much of the etched detail as possible, the artwork is scanned and edited in both 300 dpi and 1,200 dpi. Each disc comes with a browser for viewing, dragging, and placing images into various applications.

The Past-Tints brochure suggests some obvious and not so obvious ways of using the images, including letterheads, tags

284

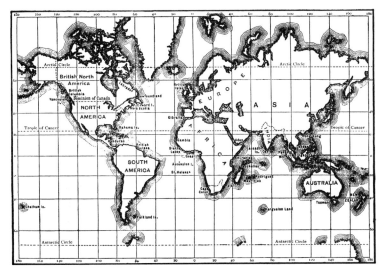

and cards, labels, fabric and paper design, magazine layouts, multimedia backgrounds, brochure covers and texture maps. It also shows a few laudable samples of the artwork in use.

285

The *Clip Art Crazy CD-ROM* includes 25 Past-Tints images in a directory labeled PERIWKLE. The files are saved in the Tagged-Image File Format (TIFF) for use with both PostScript and non-PostScript printers. The samples are the high-end 1,200 dpi versions. The file labeled READPER.WRI (in the same directory) includes the company's license agreement, which explains when and how you can use the images, along with any other information the company elected to provide.

For more information see Appendix page 356 or contact:

Periwinkle Software

7475 Brydon Rd., La Verne, CA 91750 USA

Voice: 800-730-3556, 909-593-5062; Fax: 909-593-6062,

Internet: cs@periwinkle.com

File name(s):

PER_01_B.TIF

Lilies–from the Past-Tints Sampler Edition. © 1995 Periwinkle Software. All rights reserved.

File name(s):

PER_02_B.TIF

Greenhouse–from the Past-Tints Sampler Edition. © 1995 Periwinkle Software. All rights reserved.

286

File name(s):

PER_03_B.TIF

Celery–from the Past-Tints Sampler Edition. © 1995 Periwinkle Software. All rights reserved.

File name(s):

PER_04_B.TIF

Flowers–from the Past-Tints Sampler Edition. © 1995 Periwinkle Software. All rights reserved.

File name(s):

PER_05_B.TIF

Asparagus–from the Past-Tints Sampler Edition. © 1995 Periwinkle Software. All rights reserved.

Whale–from the Past-Tints Sampler Edition. © 1995 Periwinkle Software. All rights reserved.

File name(s):
PER_06_B.TIF

Fish–from the Past-Tints Sampler Edition. © 1995 Periwinkle Software. All rights reserved.

File name(s):
PER_07_B.TIF

Warthog–from the Past-Tints Sampler Edition. © 1995 Periwinkle Software. All rights reserved.

File name(s):
PER_08_B.TIF

287

Cow–from the Past-Tints Sampler Edition. © 1995 Periwinkle Software. All rights reserved.

File name(s):
PER_09_B.TIF

Mice–from the Past-Tints Sampler Edition. © 1995 Periwinkle Software. All rights reserved.

File name(s):
PER_10_B.TIF

File name(s):

PER_11_B.TIF

Covered wagons–from the Past-Tints Sampler Edition. © 1995 Periwinkle Software. All rights reserved.

File name(s):

PER_12_B.TIF

Cottage–from the Past-Tints Sampler Edition. © 1995 Periwinkle Software. All rights reserved.

288

File name(s):

PER_13_B.TIF

Toolbox–from the Past-Tints Sampler Edition. © 1995 Periwinkle Software. All rights reserved.

File name(s):

PER_14_B.TIF

Pocket knife–from the Past-Tints Sampler Edition. © 1995 Periwinkle Software. All rights reserved.

File name(s):

PER_15_B.TIF

Biplane–from the Past-Tints Sampler Edition. © 1995 Periwinkle Software. All rights reserved.

Fox–from the Past-Tints Sampler Edition. © 1995 Periwinkle Software. All rights reserved.

File name(s):

PER_16_B.TIF

Hatbox–from the Past-Tints Sampler Edition. © 1995 Periwinkle Software. All rights reserved.

File name(s):

PER_17_B.TIF

Children and animals–from the Past-Tints Sampler Edition. © 1995 Periwinkle Software. All rights reserved.

File name(s):

PER_18_B.TIF

289

Mother and child–from the Past-Tints Sampler Edition. © 1995 Periwinkle Software. All rights reserved.

File name(s):

PER_19_B.TIF

Party–from the Past-Tints Sampler Edition. © 1995 Periwinkle Software. All rights reserved.

File name(s):

PER_20_B.TIF

File name(s):

PER_21_B.TIF

File name(s):

PER_22_B.TIF

290

File name(s):

PER_23_B.TIF

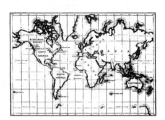

File name(s):

PER_24_B.TIF

File name(s):

PER_25_B.TIF

Chapter 22

PhotoDisc

CMCD Digital Photography

291

PhotoDisc "Clip art stinks" is the unceremonious headline on the cover of one CMCD brochure.

So says Clement Mok, the former creative director at Apple Computer, author, and founder of the renowned CMd studio. So he set out to do something about it. The result is the CMCD Digital Photography collection, a royalty-free library of visual symbols for illustration, design, advertising, desktop publishing, and presentations.

What makes the CMCD collection special is the uniqueness of the objects and the quality of the photography included. All telephones, for example, are not created equal. CMCD's old black dial phone is a cliché of a telephone. The lighting is thoughtful and the cord lays just so. While someone else might have grabbed a phone, shot it, and moved on, Mok and his staff searched out props and composed shots that define the objects they represent, producing photographs of the caliber you expect from a high-priced studio photographer. You will not find a funnier rubber chicken, a more classic piggy bank, or a more handsome wheelbarrow.

The collection includes Metaphorically Speaking, which is a library of visual puns and depictions of everyday sayings. Just Documents includes business, financial, and personal documents. Just Tools is a collection of common tools. Just Hands includes hands in different positions and holding everyday objects. And Everyday Objects is a multi-CD collection.

PhotoDisc, the company that acquired the CMCD collection and the rights to publish future titles, brings its own considerable technical skills and reputation to the table. Its current collections of objects, backgrounds, and photographic subject matter has established the company as one of the leading publishers of

292

Page 291: Lightbulb–from the CMCD Everyday Objects 2 set. Below: Mailbox–from the CMCD Visual Symbols Sampler set. © 1995 PhotoDisc Inc. All rights reserved.

digital stock photography in the business. They rescanned the original CMCD collection on high-end drum scanners, added "clipping paths" to make removing backgrounds a far simpler task, and color catalogs of the images.

The *Clip Art Crazy CD-ROM* includes 25 CMCD images in a directory labeled PHOTODSC. A low resolution version of each file is saved in the Tagged-Image File Format (TIFF) for use with both PostScript and non-PostScript printers. Five high-resolution, "print-quality" files are also included to demonstrate the ultimate image possible. The file labeled READPHT.WRI (in the same directory) includes the company's license agreement, which explains when and how you can use the images, along with any other information the company elected to provide.

For more information see Appendix page 357 or contact:
PhotoDisc Inc.

2013 Fourth Ave., Seattle, WA 98121 USA

Voice: 800-528-3472, 206-441-9355; Fax: 206-441-9379

E-mail: sales@photodisc.com

Internet: http://www.photodisc.com

File name(s):
PHT_01_C.TIF

Cornet, trumpet–from the CMCD Everyday Objects 3 set. © 1995 PhotoDisc Inc. All rights reserved.

File name(s):
PHT_02_C.TIF

Dollar bill–from the CMCD Just Documents set. © 1995 PhotoDisc Inc. All rights reserved.

294

File name(s):
PHT_03_C.TIF
PHT_03_H.TIF

Globe–from the CMCD Everyday Objects 1 set. © 1995 PhotoDisc Inc. All rights reserved. The second file is a high-resolution version.

File name(s):
PHT_04_C.TIF

Life preserver–from the CMCD Metaphorically Speaking set. © 1995 PhotoDisc Inc. All rights reserved.

File name(s):
PHT_05_C.TIF

Lightbulb–from the CMCD Everyday Objects 2 set. © 1995 PhotoDisc Inc. All rights reserved.

Pilot's hat and sunglasses–from the CMCD Everyday Objects 1 set. © 1995 PhotoDisc Inc. All rights reserved.

File name(s):

PHT_06_C.TIF

Rubber chicken–from the CMCD Just Hands set. © 1995 PhotoDisc Inc. All rights reserved.

File name(s):

PHT_07_C.TIF

CD-ROM–from the CMCD Just Hands set. © 1995 PhotoDisc Inc. All rights reserved. The second file is a high-resolution version.

File name(s):

PHT_08_C.TIF

PHT_08_H.TIF

295

Scale–from the CMCD Just Tools set. © 1995 PhotoDisc Inc. All rights reserved.

File name(s):

PHT_09_C.TIF

Nest–from the CMCD Everyday Objects 2 set. © 1995 PhotoDisc Inc. All rights reserved.

File name(s):

PHT_10_C.TIF

File name(s):
PHT_11_C.TIF

Telephone–from the CMCD Just Tools set. © 1995 PhotoDisc Inc. All rights reserved.

File name(s):
PHT_12_C.TIF

Piggy bank–from the CMCD Everyday Objects 1 set. © 1995 PhotoDisc Inc. All rights reserved.

296

File name(s):
PHT_13_C.TIF

Eyeglasses–from the CMCD Everyday Objects 2 set. © 1995 PhotoDisc Inc. All rights reserved.

File name(s):
PHT_14_C.TIF
PHT_14_H.TIF

Dog–from the CMCD Everyday Objects 2 set. © 1995 PhotoDisc Inc. All rights reserved. The second file is a high-resolution version.

File name(s):
PHT_15_C.TIF

Fortune cookie–from the CMCD Metaphorically Speaking set. © 1995 PhotoDisc Inc. All rights reserved.

Bingo card–from the CMCD Just Documents set. © 1995 PhotoDisc Inc. All rights reserved.

File name(s):

PHT_16_C.TIF

Film reel–from the CMCD Everyday Objects 2 set. © 1995 PhotoDisc Inc. All rights reserved.

File name(s):

PHT_17_C.TIF

Bicycle–from the CMCD Everyday Objects 2 set. © 1995 PhotoDisc Inc. All rights reserved. The second file is a high-resolution version.

File name(s):

PHT_18_C.TIF

PHT_18_H.TIF

297

Basketball–from the CMCD Everyday Objects 2 set. © 1995 PhotoDisc Inc. All rights reserved.

File name(s):

PHT_19_C.TIF

Rotary card file–from the CMCD Just Tools set. © 1995 PhotoDisc Inc. All rights reserved.

File name(s):

PHT_20_C.TIF

File name(s):
PHT_21_C.TIF

Pen–from the CMCD Everyday Objects 2 set. © 1995 PhotoDisc Inc. All rights reserved.

File name(s):
PHT_22_C.TIF

Half-full glass–from the CMCD Metaphorically Speaking set. © 1995 PhotoDisc Inc. All rights reserved.

298

File name(s):
PHT_23_C.TIF

Hot water bottle–from the CMCD Everyday Objects 1 set. © 1995 PhotoDisc Inc. All rights reserved.

File name(s):
PHT_24_C.TIF

Sheet music–from the CMCD Visual Symbols Sampler set. © 1995 PhotoDisc Inc. All rights reserved.

File name(s):
PHT_25_C.TIF
PHT_25_H.TIF

Mailbox–from the CMCD Visual Symbols Sampler set. © 1995 PhotoDisc Inc. All rights reserved. The second file is a high-resolution version.

Chapter 23

T/Maker Company

ClickArt

T/Maker Company Hiedi Roizen and T/Maker helped pioneer the electronic clip art business with ClickArt.

T/Maker and CEO Roizen have, as a matter of fact, taken the lead on a number of fronts—in 1979 with one of the original spreadsheet programs, in 1984 with the first software products for Apple's Macintosh, and 1986 with one of the first desktop publishing products for the PC, First Publisher.

The ClickArt clip art series, with over 30 titles, is among the leading brands of clip art marketed today. Titles include ClickArt Cartoons featuring Beastly Funnies, On the Job, Bulletins & Newsletters, and other categories; ClickArt Studio Series featuring Artistry & Borders, Sports & Games, Business Art, and others; and The Incredible Image Pak 25,000, a collection of 25,000 images covering a variety of subjects.

In addition to its own creations, T/Maker markets the work of other illustrators and cartoonists under the ClickArt flag. Famous Magazine Cartoons, for one, includes the work of nine editorial cartoonists whose work has appeared in publications as wide reaching as the *Wall Street Journal*, the *Washington Post*, and *The New Yorker*. It would be no small feat otherwise to include the wit and wisdom of nationally recognized artists such as Charles Barsotti, Harley Schwadron, or Al Ross in your company newsletter.

All of the ClickArt collections feature The ClickArt Trade Secret, a utility that converts files to your choice of file formats, including EPS, AI, CGM, WMF, PCX, TIFF, and even the proprietary format used with Broderbund's Print Shop Deluxe.

The *Clip Art Crazy CD-ROM* includes 25 ClickArt images in a directory labeled TMAKER. The files are saved as both PostScript (EPS) files for use with PostScript printers and as Windows Metafiles (WMF) for use with non-PostScript printers. The file labeled READTMK.WRI (in the same directory) includes the company's license agreement, which explains when and how you can use the images, along with any other information the company elected to provide.

For more information see Appendix page 358 or contact:

T/Maker Company

1390 Villa St., Mountain View, CA 94041 USA

Voice: 800-9TMAKER, (800-986-2537), 415-962-0195;

Fax: 415-962-0201

Internet: click_art@tmaker.com

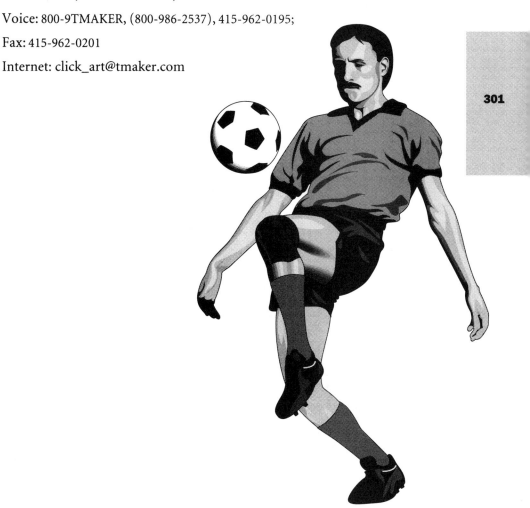

Soccer–from the ClickArt Studio Series Sports & Games portfolio. © 1995 T/Maker Company. All rights reserved worldwide. ClickArt and T/Maker are registered trademarks of T/Maker Company.

301

File name(s):
TMK_01_C.EPS
TMK_01_C.WMF

Lighthouse–from the ClickArt Christian Illustrations portfolio. © 1995 T/Maker Company. All rights reserved worldwide.

File name(s):
TMK_02_B.EPS
TMK_02_B.WMF

Rabbit–from the ClickArt Artistry & Borders portfolio. © 1995 T/Maker Company. All rights reserved worldwide.

File name(s):
TMK_03_B.EPS
TMK_03_B.WMF

Compass–from the ClickArt Studio Series Artistry & Borders portfolio. © 1995 T/Maker Company. All rights reserved worldwide.

File name(s):
TMK_04_B.EPS
TMK_04_B.WMF

Running–from the ClickArt Newsletter Art portfolio. © 1995 T/Maker Company. All rights reserved worldwide.

File name(s):
TMK_05_B.EPS
TMK_05_B.WMF

Telephone–from the ClickArt Studio Series Artistry & Borders portfolio. © 1995 T/Maker Company. All rights reserved worldwide.

Town–from the ClickArt Christian Illustrations portfolio. © 1995 T/Maker Company. All rights reserved worldwide.

File name(s):

TMK_06_C.EPS

TMK_06_C.WMF

Sailboat–from the ClickArt Studio Series Business Art portfolio. © 1995 T/Maker Company. All rights reserved worldwide.

File name(s):

TMK_07_B.EPS

TMK_07_B.WMF

Magnifying glass–from the ClickArt Studio Series Business Art portfolio. © 1995 T/Maker Company. All rights reserved worldwide.

File name(s):

TMK_08_B.EPS

TMK_08_B.WMF

303

Pencil–from the ClickArt Studio Series Business Art portfolio. © 1995 T/Maker Company. All rights reserved worldwide.

File name(s):

TMK_09_C.EPS

TMK_09_C.WMF

Map of Europe–from the ClickArt Business Illustrations portfolio. © 1995 T/Maker Company. All rights reserved worldwide.

File name(s):

TMK_10_C.EPS

TMK_10_C.WMF

File name(s):

TMK_11_B.EPS

TMK_11_B.WMF

Rat–from the ClickArt Beastly Funny Cartoons portfolio. © 1995 T/Maker Company. All rights reserved worldwide.

File name(s):

TMK_12_B.EPS

TMK_12_B.WMF

Mail–from the ClickArt On the Job Cartoons portfolio. © 1995 T/Maker Company. All rights reserved worldwide.

File name(s):

TMK_13_B.EPS

TMK_13_B.WMF

Electronic mail–from the ClickArt On the Job Cartoons portfolio. © 1995 T/Maker Company. All rights reserved worldwide.

File name(s):

TMK_14_B.EPS

TMK_14_B.WMF

Barbeque–from the ClickArt Parties & Events Cartoons portfolio. © 1995 T/Maker Company. All rights reserved worldwide.

File name(s):

TMK_15_B.EPS

TMK_15_B.WMF

Life preserver–from the ClickArt Company & Business Cartoons portfolio. © 1995 T/Maker Company. All rights reserved worldwide.

Giraffe–from the ClickArt Animals & Nature Studio Series portfolio. © 1995 T/Maker Company. All rights reserved worldwide.	*File name(s):* TMK_16_C.EPS TMK_16_C.WMF	
Sun–from the ClickArt Studio Series Artistry & Borders portfolio. © 1995 T/Maker Company. All rights reserved worldwide.	*File name(s):* TMK_17_B.EPS TMK_17_B.WMF	
Soccer field layout–from the ClickArt Studio Series Sports & Games portfolio. © 1995 T/Maker Company. All rights reserved worldwide.	*File name(s):* TMK_18_B.EPS TMK_18_B.WMF	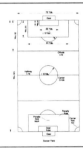
Star–from the ClickArt Occasions & Celebrations portfolio. © 1995 T/Maker Company. All rights reserved worldwide.	*File name(s):* TMK_19_C.EPS TMK_19_C.WMF	
"at" symbol–from the ClickArt Studio Series Artistry & Borders portfolio. © 1995 T/Maker Company. All rights reserved worldwide.	*File name(s):* TMK_20_B.EPS TMK_20_B.WMF	

File name(s):
TMK_21_C.EPS
TMK_21_C.WMF

Milk carton–from the ClickArt Studio Series Artistry & Borders portfolio. © 1995 T/Maker Company. All rights reserved worldwide.

File name(s):
TMK_22_B.EPS
TMK_22_B.WMF

Pig–from the ClickArt Studio Series Artistry & Borders portfolio. © 1995 T/Maker Company. All rights reserved worldwide.

File name(s):
TMK_23_B.EPS
TMK_23_B.WMF

Flower–from the ClickArt Studio Series Artistry & Borders portfolio. © 1995 T/Maker Company. All rights reserved worldwide.

306

File name(s):
TMK_24_B.EPS
TMK_24_B.WMF

Running–from ClickArt 101. © 1995 T/Maker Company. All rights reserved worldwide.

File name(s):
TMK_25_C.EPS
TMK_25_C.WMF

Gavel–from the ClickArt Studio Series Business Art portfolio. © 1995 T/Maker Company. All rights reserved worldwide.

Chapter 24

Ultimate Symbol

Design Elements-A Digital Reference

Ultimate Symbol A good visual symbol is complex, but the complexity is not obvious.

Flourishes, accents, devices, symbols, designs, shapes, and ornaments are the designer's attempt to reduce ideas and feelings to basic visual form. Design Elements-A Digital Reference is a museum-quality collection of over 3,200 of these complex images, 50 years in the making.

Over their combined design careers Richard and Mies Hora, father and son, have built a huge archive of basic visual forms. Richard had researched and developed hundreds of images over his 40 years as an artist and architect and collected a sizable collection of specimens from old books, nineteenth-century linecuts, German type specimens, and other sources. Mies, a recognized designer in his own right, augmented the archive by expanding the categories and contributing new material and ideas.

Between 1980 and 1985, the two published the archive as a series of best-selling design reference books, *Design Elements - A Visual Reference.* The four volumes were recognized by graphics experts for their scope and quality. Now, over a decade later, a newly edited and expanded version of the archive has emerged. The symbols are now in digital form— pristine PostScript files (the samples on the *Clip Art Crazy CD-ROM* are also in Windows Metafiles [WMF]).

Categories include Pictorial Symbols, Motifs-Shapes-Design Devices, Printer's Ornaments-Dingbat Designs, Arrows-Pointers, Flourishes-Accents-Typographic Devices, Circular Designs, and Shapes-Designs-Geometrics.

Page 307: Fingerprint–from Volume 3-Pictorial Symbols. Above: Compass rose–from Volume 7-Circular Designs of Design Elements-A Digital Reference. © 1995 Ultimate Symbol Inc. All rights reserved.

A screen catalog of all 3,200 images stored in an Adobe Acrobat file (PDF) is included on the *Clip Art Crazy CD-ROM*. Acrobat allows you to view all of the images even though you do not have access to the actual files. A discussion of how to view and/or print the book is included in the READUSI.WRI file described below.

The *Clip Art Crazy CD-ROM* includes 25 images from *Design Elements* in a directory labeled ULTIMSYM. The files are saved as both PostScript (EPS) files for use with PostScript printers and as Windows Metafiles (WMF) for use with non-PostScript printers. The file labeled READUSI.WRI (in the same directory) includes the company's license agreement, which explains when and how you can use the images, along with any other information the company elected to provide.

Trees–from Volume 3- Pictorial Symbols of Design Elements-A Digital Reference. © 1995 Ultimate Symbol Inc. All rights reserved.

For more information see Appendix page 359 or contact:

Ultimate Symbol Inc.

31 Wilderness Dr., Stony Point, NY 10980 USA

Voice: 800-870-7940, Fax: 914-942-0004

File name(s):
USI_01_B.EPS
USI_01_B.WMF

Star–from Volume 1-Stars-Suns-Moons-Zodiac of Design Elements. © 1995 Ultimate Symbol Inc. All rights reserved.

File name(s):
USI_02_B.EPS
USI_02_B.WMF

Sun–from Volume 1-Stars-Suns-Moons-Zodiac of Design Elements. © 1995 Ultimate Symbol Inc. All rights reserved.

310

File name(s):
USI_03_B.EPS
USI_03_B.WMF

Correct hand signal–from Volume 3-Pictorial Symbols of Design Elements. © 1995 Ultimate Symbol Inc. All rights reserved.

File name(s):
USI_04_B.EPS
USI_04_B.WMF

Face–from Volume 1-Stars-Suns-Moons-Zodiac of Design Elements. © 1995 Ultimate Symbol Inc. All rights reserved.

File name(s):
USI_05_B.EPS
USI_05_B.WMF

Dart board–from Volume 7-Circular Designs of Design Elements. © 1995 Ultimate Symbol Inc. All rights reserved.

Ornament–from Volume 2-Flourishes-Accents-Typographic Devices of Design Elements. © 1995 Ultimate Symbol Inc. All rights reserved.	*File name(s):* USI_06_B.EPS USI_06_B.WMF	
Globe–from Volume 7-Circular Designs of Design Elements. © 1995 Ultimate Symbol Inc. All rights reserved.	*File name(s):* USI_07_B.EPS USI_07_B.WMF	
Swan–from Volume 3-Pictorial Symbols of Design Elements. © 1995 Ultimate Symbol Inc. All rights reserved.	*File name(s):* USI_08_B.EPS USI_08_B.WMF	
Ornament–from Volume 2-Flourishes-Accents-Typographic Devices of Design Elements. © 1995 Ultimate Symbol Inc. All rights reserved.	*File name(s):* USI_09_B.EPS USI_09_B.WMF	
Dagger–from Volume 6-Arrows-Pointers of Design Elements. © 1995 Ultimate Symbol Inc. All rights reserved.	*File name(s):* USI_10_B.EPS USI_10_B.WMF	

311

File name(s):
USI_11_B.EPS
USI_11_B.WMF

*Spiral–from Volume 7-
Circular Designs of
Design Elements.
© 1995 Ultimate
Symbol Inc. All rights
reserved.*

File name(s):
USI_12_B.EPS
USI_12_B.WMF

*Stamp–from Volume 4-
Motifs-Shapes-Designs-
Devices of Design
Elements.
© 1995 Ultimate
Symbol Inc. All rights
reserved.*

312

File name(s):
USI_13_B.EPS
USI_13_B.WMF

*Wheat–from Volume 5-
Printers' Ornaments-
Dingbats-Designs of
Design Elements.
© 1995 Ultimate
Symbol Inc. All rights
reserved.*

File name(s):
USI_14_B.EPS
USI_14_B.WMF

*Lips–from Volume 3-
Pictorial Symbols of
Design Elements.
© 1995 Ultimate
Symbol Inc. All rights
reserved.*

File name(s):
USI_15_B.EPS
USI_15_B.WMF

*Arrow–from Volume 6-
Arrows Pointers of
Design Elements.
© 1995 Ultimate
Symbol Inc. All rights
reserved.*

Ornament–from Volume 5-Printers' Ornaments-Dingbats-Designs of Design Elements. © 1995 Ultimate Symbol Inc. All rights reserved.	*File name(s):* USI_16_B.EPS USI_16_B.WMF	
Leaf–from Volume 3-Pictorial Symbols of Design Elements. © 1995 Ultimate Symbol Inc. All rights reserved.	*File name(s):* USI_17_B.EPS USI_17_B.WMF	
Compass rose–from Volume 7-Circular Designs of Design Elements. © 1995 Ultimate Symbol Inc. All rights reserved.	*File name(s):* USI_18_B.EPS USI_18_B.WMF	
Puzzle piece–from Volume 8-Shapes-Designs-Geometrics of Design Elements. © 1995 Ultimate Symbol Inc. All rights reserved.	*File name(s):* USI_19_B.EPS USI_19_B.WMF	
Lion–from Volume 6-Arrows Pointers of Design Elements. © 1995 Ultimate Symbol Inc. All rights reserved.	*File name(s):* USI_20_B.EPS USI_20_B.WMF	

File name(s):
USI_21_B.EPS
USI_21_B.WMF

Baby–from Volume 3-Pictorial Symbols of Design Elements.
© 1995 Ultimate Symbol Inc. All rights reserved.

File name(s):
USI_22_B.EPS
USI_22_B.WMF

Ornament–from Volume 7-Circular Designs of Design Elements. © 1995 Ultimate Symbol Inc. All rights reserved.

314

File name(s):
USI_23_B.EPS
USI_23_B.WMF

Snowflake–from Volume 7-Circular Designs of Design Elements. © 1995 Ultimate Symbol Inc. All rights reserved.

File name(s):
USI_24_B.EPS
USI_24_B.WMF

Gem–from Volume 8-Shapes-Designs-Geometrics of Design Elements. © 1995 Ultimate Symbol Inc. All rights reserved.

File name(s):
USI_25_B.EPS
USI_25_B.WMF

Quilt symbol–from Volume 5-Printers' Ornaments-Dingbats-Designs of Design Elements. © 1995 Ultimate Symbol Inc. All rights reserved.

Chapter 25

Youth
Specialties

ArtSource

Youth Specialties The Lord works in mysterious ways.

Dave Adamson and his company, The Church Art Works, prove that radical art and attitudes can be a positive, uplifting force. In addition to a wide selection of digital and conventional cut and paste clip art titles, The Church Art Works

licenses its signature style graphics to Christian-oriented apparel, card, and poster manufacturers that market their designs around the world.

The company has both a mission and a ministry. The mission is "to present Christ through quality" by doing the research and legwork necessary to stay current with the look and the language of teens and young adults. The ministry is to produce products and services that deliver the tenets of the Christian faith to the youth they serve.

Youth Specialties is the exclusive publisher of the The Church Art Works' Art Source Clip Art Series. The products fit well within the mix of nondenominational teaching and training tools, publications, and products they have compiled over 25 years of serving youth ministries.

The illustrations styles run the gamut—cartoons, woodblocks, photocollage, and even a few straight, business-like drawings. While the religious significance of some images is obvious, there are many that could be used in general desktop publishing projects. Titles include Fantastic Activities, Attention Getters, Sports, Amazing Oddities, Appalling Images, Spiritual Topics, and others.

316

Page 315: Hair–from ArtSource Volume Five-Amazing Oddities and Appalling Images. Above: Sun–from ArtSource Volume Two-Borders, Symbols, Holidays, and Attention Getters. © 1995 Youth Specialties, Inc. All rights reserved.

The *Clip Art Crazy CD-ROM* includes 25 ArtSource images in a directory labeled YOUTHSPC. The files are saved in the Tagged-Image File Format (TIFF) for use with both PostScript and non-PostScript printers. The file labeled READYSP.WRI (in the same directory) includes the company's license agreement, which explains when and how you can use the images, along with any other information the company elected to provide.

For more information see Appendix page 360 or contact:

Youth Specialties, Inc.

P.O. Box 4406, Spartanburg, SC 29305 USA

Voice: 800-776-8008, 803-573-7004; Fax: 803-583-7381

Internet: youthspec@aol.com

Above: Skiing–from ArtSource Volume One-Fantastic Activities. Below: Deer–from ArtSource Volume Two-Borders, Symbols, Holidays, and Attention Getters. © 1995 Youth Specialties, Inc. All rights reserved.

File name(s):
YSP_01_B.TIF

Young man on telephone–from ArtSource Volume Two-Borders, Symbols, Holidays, and Attention Getters. © 1995 Youth Specialties Inc. All rights reserved.

File name(s):
YSP_02_B.TIF

Young woman on telephone–from ArtSource Volume Two-Borders, Symbols, Holidays, and Attention Getters. © 1995 Youth Specialties Inc. All rights reserved.

318

File name(s):
YSP_03_B.TIF

Young woman on telephone–from ArtSource Volume Two-Borders, Symbols, Holidays, and Attention Getters. © 1995 Youth Specialties Inc. All rights reserved.

File name(s):
YSP_04_B.TIF

Bible–from ArtSource Volume Two-Borders, Symbols, Holidays, and Attention Getters. © 1995 Youth Specialties Inc. All rights reserved.

File name(s):
YSP_05_B.TIF

Picnic–from ArtSource Volume One-Fantastic Activities. © 1995 Youth Specialties Inc. All rights reserved.

Camping–from Artsource Volume One-Fantastic Activities. © 1995 Youth Specialties Inc. All rights reserved.

File name(s):

YSP_06_B.TIF

Graduation–from ArtSource Volume One-Fantastic Activities. © 1995 Youth Specialties Inc. All rights reserved.

File name(s):

YSP_07_B.TIF

Rafting–from ArtSource Volume One-Fantastic Activities. © 1995 Youth Specialties Inc. All rights reserved.

File name(s):

YSP_08_B.TIF

319

Basketball–from ArtSource Volume Three-Sports. © 1995 Youth Specialties Inc. All rights reserved.

File name(s):

YSP_09_B.TIF

Volleyball–from ArtSource Volume Three-Sports. © 1995 Youth Specialties Inc. All rights reserved.

File name(s):

YSP_10_B.TIF

	File name(s): YSP_11_B.TIF	*Running–from ArtSource Volume Three-Sports. © 1995 Youth Specialties Inc. All rights reserved.*
	File name(s): YSP_12_B.TIF	*Racquetball–from ArtSource Volume Three-Sports. © 1995 Youth Specialties Inc. All rights reserved.*
	File name(s): YSP_13_B.TIF	*Baseball player–from ArtSource Volume Three-Sports. © 1995 Youth Specialties Inc. All rights reserved.*
	File name(s): YSP_14_B.TIF	*Hair–from ArtSource Volume Five-Amazing Oddities and Appalling Images. © 1995 Youth Specialties Inc. All rights reserved.*
	File name(s): YSP_15_B.TIF	*Straightjacket–from ArtSource Volume Five-Amazing Oddities and Appalling Images. © 1995 Youth Specialties Inc. All rights reserved.*

320

Bush baby–from ArtSource Volume Five-Amazing Oddities and Appalling Images. © 1995 Youth Specialties Inc. All rights reserved.

File name(s):

YSP_16_B.TIF

Motorcycle policeman– from ArtSource Volume Five-Amazing Oddities and Appalling Images. © 1995 Youth Specialties Inc. All rights reserved.

File name(s):

YSP_17_B.TIF

Face–from ArtSource Volume Five-Amazing Oddities and Appalling Images. © 1995 Youth Specialties Inc. All rights reserved.

File name(s):

YSP_18_B.TIF

321

Pottery wheel–from ArtSource Volume Six-Spiritual Topics. © 1995 Youth Specialties Inc. All rights reserved.

File name(s):

YSP_19_B.TIF

Tough choices–from ArtSource Volume Six-Spiritual Topics. © 1995 Youth Specialties Inc. All rights reserved.

File name(s):

YSP_20_B.TIF

File name(s):
YSP_21_B.TIF

Garbage in garbage out– from ArtSource Volume Six-Spiritual Topics. © 1995 Youth Specialties Inc. All rights reserved.

File name(s):
YSP_22_B.TIF

Tearing down the walls– from ArtSource Volume Six-Spiritual Topics. © 1995 Youth Specialties Inc. All rights reserved.

322

File name(s):
YSP_23_B.TIF

Marshmallows–from Volume One-Fantastic Activities. © 1995 Youth Specialties Inc. All rights reserved.

File name(s):
YSP_24_B.TIF

Good job–from ArtSource Volume Four-Phrases and Verses. © 1995 Youth Specialties Inc. All rights reserved.

File name(s):
YSP_25_B.TIF

Takin' it to the streets-the Gospel–from Volume Four-Phrases and Verses. © 1995 Youth Specialties Inc. All rights reserved.

Appendix

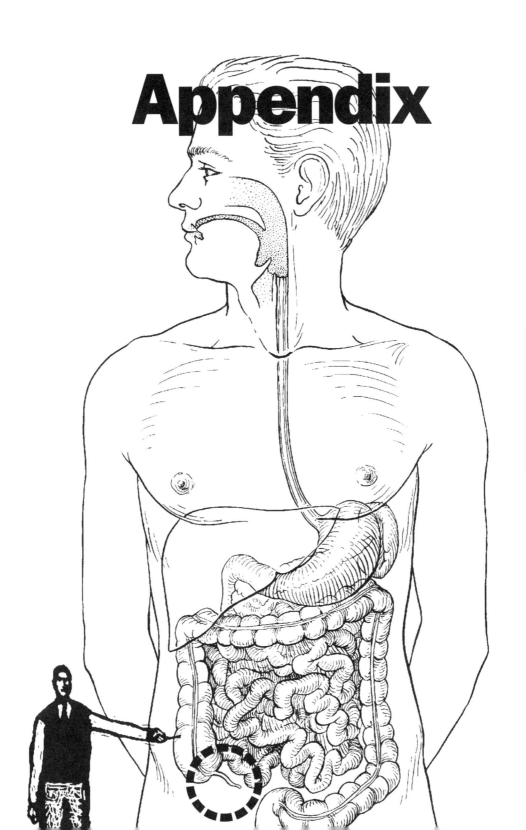

Enough said. Time to allow the companies who contributed to *Clip Art Crazy* and the CD-ROM to speak for themselves.

On the pages that follow you'll find information provided by the 20 companies you read about in Chapters 6 through 25. Be sure to check out the coupons on the page corners for special offers for *Clip Art Crazy* readers.

Aridi Computer Graphics Library

P.O. Box 797702, Dallas, Texas 75379, Voice: 214-404-9171; Fax: 214-404-9172

1-800-755-6441

Volumes 1 through 5 CD-ROM, Version 2.0 $399.00

Over 450 meg of information. This hybrid CD-ROM (for both Mac & PC) contains every image in Volumes 1 through 5. An excellent resource for decorative borders, ornaments or initial capital letters with an elegant antique look.

Volumes 1 & 2–Initial Caps–Twelve sets of initial cap font graphics with every letter from A-Z in color and black and white. The origins of these designs are illuminated manuscripts from various eras–from the Middle Ages to the Renaissance.

Volume 3–Historic Ornaments, Patterns & Frames–Features a large selection of full frames, motifs and patterns adopted from manuscripts, tiles, carved wood panels, textiles and wallpaper created mostly in Europe during the Victorian era.

Volume 4–Arabesque Ornaments–A large selection of medallions and motifs that provide a unique new approach to reproducing the intricate geometric and floral interlacing of book covers from ancient times.

Volume 5–Arabesque Borders–The characteristic that distinguishes Arabesque decoration from that of other great civilizations is the predominantly geometric nature of the ornament.

(Mac users can purchase the CD-ROM of a HD diskette version of individual Volumes 1 through 5 for $129.00 each. PC users should purchase the Version 2.0 CD-ROM.)

327

Volume 6–Olde World Borders I CD-ROM $149.00

Aridi's latest release of decorative borders from around the world. Offering 200 designs: Celtic, Arabesque, Art Deco, Victorian, Calligraphy and Decorative Corners are all represented. As always, for ease of design, the images are hand-drawn with strict attention to detail in both Black & White and CMYK.

Volume 7–Initial Caps III CD-ROM $149.00

Six different initial capital letter designs of twenty-six letters each. "Masselle," inspired by a fifteenth century Italian designer, "Vincente," inspired by a seventeeth-century Italian designer. "Rosettes, Cherubs, Victoriana and Fantasia" are all representative of the floral, ornate Victorian era. File formats offered include, EPS, FreeHand, and PICT for the Mac, and .EPS, CorelDRAW!, and .BMP for the PC.

Special offer for Clip Art Crazy readers!

Get 25% off these prices or buy all three CD-ROMs for only $399.00!
To take advantage of this offer you must order direct from Aridi Computer Graphics at our toll-free number: 800-755-6441.

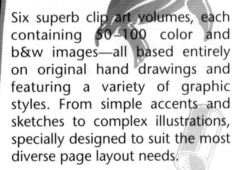
328

329

Is your Clip Art a Little Stale?

Freshen it up with MEGATOONS!

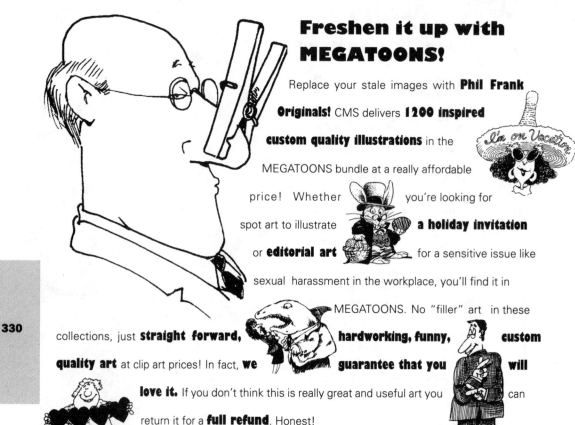

Replace your stale images with **Phil Frank Originals!** CMS delivers **1200 inspired custom quality illustrations** in the MEGATOONS bundle at a really affordable price! Whether you're looking for spot art to illustrate **a holiday invitation** or **editorial art** for a sensitive issue like sexual harassment in the workplace, you'll find it in MEGATOONS. No "filler" art in these collections, just **straight forward, hardworking, funny, custom quality art** at clip art prices! In fact, **we guarantee that you will love it.** If you don't think this is really great and useful art you can return it for a **full refund**. Honest!

330

PLEASE SEND ME:

❑ **MEGATOONS PART I** — **$99⁹⁵**
   ❑ CD-ROM   ❑ MAC Disks   ❑ PC Disks (3.5")

❑ **MEGATOONS PART II** — **$99⁹⁵**
   ❑ CD-ROM   ❑ MAC Disks   ❑ PC Disks (3.5")

❑ **MEGATOONS BUNDLE** — **$179⁹⁵**
   (Part I and Part II)
   ❑ CD-ROM (Part I and Part II on one CD ROM)
   ❑ MAC Disks   ❑ PC Disks (3.5")

   U.S. shipping add $4.95 / Canadian shipping add $6.95
   ORDER TOTAL (CA residents add sales tax):

$ _____

Clip Art Crazy
readers: 15% OFF
Megatoons Bundle with
this proof of purchase.
Call: 800-358-2278

Method of payment:
❑ Payment enclosed (Must be in U.S. dollars)
❑ Please charge my credit card
   ❑ Visa   ❑ MasterCard   ❑ Amer. Express
Card number _____
Expiration date _____
Authorizing signature _____

SEND TO THE ATTENTION OF:
Name _____
Company _____
Address _____
(Full address please—we cannot ship to a P.O. Box)
City_____ State _____ Zip _____

CMS • P.O. Box 5955 • Berkeley, CA 94705
(800) 358-2278 • (510) 843-3408 • FAX (510) 549-2490

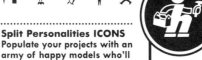

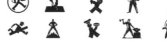

332

Clip Art Crazy
readers:
Call 1-800-297-7658
for a FREE CATALOG

Look no further!

Eye Catching Spot Illustrations from Letraset®

336

FONTEK
Design Fonts™

21 collections of spot illustrations in font format. Each collection of DesignFonts contains dozens of graphic images that range from medieval drawings to funky high-tech objects.

DesignFonts are unique, cutting edge designs that are upmost in quality. They give the designer the ability to add bold new flair to a design, with a popular look that is sure to be noticed. Packed with a wide range for styles, topics and designs. DesignFonts are economical too, costing $1 per image as compared to $100 for an illustrator. They can be easily manipulated like any other typeface to adjust size, spacing, style and alignment. You can stretch, color, outline, and shadow them. Also, because DesignFonts are in font format, they take up much less memory than yesterday's clip art.

DesignFonts are available for both the Macintosh™ and IBM compatible computers. Call (800) 343-TYPE for a free specifier.

Letraset®
40 Eisenhower Drive
Paramus, NJ 07653

Macintosh is a trademark of
Apple Computer Incorporated.

Clip Art Crazy
readers: Call
800-343-TYPE
for a free specifier

THE WORKS

CREATIVE GRAPHICS, INC.

- *Metro® Newspaper Service*
- *Classified Dynamics®*
- *Sales Spectaculars™*
- *Holiday Advertising Service*
- *AdCreation Toolkit™*

33 West 34th Street
New York, NY 10001
800-223-1600

Gear Up For Profits With Metro!

From ideas and concepts through sales and production, Metro offers hardworking, creative solutions that can build big advertising profits for you. Each of Metro's art and idea services, as well as the exciting new AdCreation Toolkit™ for QuarkXPress® users, is the result of continuous customer input and reflects 85+ years in the advertising and publishing industry. Designed specifically for the way you do business, each product is geared to your needs, now and for the future!

CREATIVE SALES AND PRODUCTION POWER FROM METRO

338

339

THE FINEST DIGITAL ART AVAILABLE FOR PROFESSIONAL DESIGNERS

O · S · W · E · G · O
ILLUSTRATED ARCHIVES

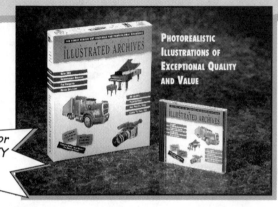

OVER 350 INCOMPARABLE GRAPHICS

FOR UNLIMITED DESIGN SOLUTIONS

ON CD-ROM

ONLY $179.95

Special price for CLIP ART CRAZY customers $49.95

PHOTOREALISTIC ILLUSTRATIONS OF EXCEPTIONAL QUALITY AND VALUE

MORE THAN JUST ANOTHER "CLIP ART" COLLECTION, each illustration on the *Oswego Illustrated Archives* CD-ROM is a meticulously crafted masterpiece. Created with the attention to quality, flexibility, and detail you'd expect from a world leader in digital graphics.

Illustrations on this CD-ROM are saved in EPS format and can be imported into page layout programs that accept EPS files. You can print them in a variety of sizes or resolutions without compromising their exceptional detail. With Adobe Illustrator,® you can even customize the files for your own specific needs.

Files on the *Oswego Illustrated Archives* CD-ROM are organized into the following categories:

- Architectural Elements
- Business
- Flora & Fauna
- Food
- Hardware
- Home Appliances
- Home Electronics
- Mobile Electronics
- Musical Instruments
- Sports
- Transportation

EPS FILES OF EXCEPTIONAL DETAIL

MACINTOSH® & WINDOWS® COMPATIBLE

Featuring KUDO™ Image Browser For Macintosh Version

OSWEGO COMPANY

Portland, Oregon
Phone: (503) 274-9338 • Fax: (503) 274-9326

ORDER NOW! 1-800-275-1989

© 1993 The Oswego Company. All rights reserved. Printed in USA. Registered trademarks are the property of their respective companies.

Clip Art Crazy readers: Mention this offer and get the Oswego Illustrated Archives CD-ROM for just $49.95!

Clip Art Crazy readers:
Call: 212-941-7418
Fax: 212-431-7138

Rendered with Devotion and Understanding, Variations on
a Core Collection of Essential Symbols by Daniel Pelavin
Facsimile: 212 431-7138 • Telephone: 212 941-7418
Daniel Pelavin 80 Varick Street #3B New York City 10013
http://www.inch.com/~dpelavin/

341

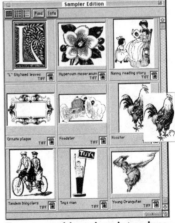

343

A w a r d   W i n n i n g   I m a g e s | M a c U s e r   E d d y   A w a r d s

PhotoDisc Starter Kit

Preview PhotoDisc for only $29! (Only when you mention this book–regularly $39). Over 9,000 low-res images plus 25 high-res images. You also get this 256 page image reference book. An incredible value!

 1994

- Royalty free for marketing, advertising, multimedia and more.

- High resolution for full page layouts.

 1993

- Ready for color or B&W printing or laser output.

- Artistic and technical quality makes PhotoDisc the 10 to 1 favorite.

 1992 **Call today! T: 1 800 528.3472 / F: 1 206 441 9379**

Call for your free brochure today! 1-800-9-TMAKER

ARTSOURCE™
The ultimate youth ministry clip art series

The Church Art Works

You know how clip art adds fun and energy to your promotions. Here's the best youth ministry clip art around! Seven volumes filled with the latest designs are available in books or on computer disk. Plus you'll get design tips from the pros to help transform even the simplest piece into a masterpiece. Use for—

- ➤ Calendars
- ➤ Newsletters
- ➤ Overheads
- ➤ Fliers
- ➤ Postcards
- ➤ Posters

➤ **Volume One: Fantastic Activities**
Designs for socials, retreats, game nights, special events
➤ **Volume Two: Borders, Symbols, Holidays, and Attention Getters**
Creative designs, logos, and illustrations to liven up your promotional materials
➤ **Volume Three: Sports**
Easy-to-use clip art for volleyball, basketball, baseball, soccer, football, and more
➤ **Volume Four: Phrases & Verses**
Phrases and Scripture verses for newsletters, brochures, and fliers
➤ **Volume Five: Amazing Oddities and Appalling Images**
The most hilarious, crazy, and downright bizarre clip art you've ever seen
➤ **Volume Six: Spiritual Topics**
Topical and thematic clip art for your teaching series, camp and retreat themes, and more
➤ **NEW! Variety Pack (Volume Seven)**
Ready-to-use clip art that covers a variety of topics
Note: Volume seven not available on disk...available early 1996 on CDROM!

ArtSource Books

➤ **Individual books** (Specify Volume ASB#) .... **$10.99 each**
➤ **Complete ArtSource set of seven books**
    (ASBSET) .... Reg. ~~$76.93~~
                                                          Only $65.99

Computer Disks
Also available on Computer Disk for using on your IBM or MAC!

➤ **Individual ArtSource volume**
    (specify IBM or Mac and Volume #) .... **$49.99 each**

Computer specs: Images are digitized at 300 dpi in Tagged Image File Format (TIFF), which are in black & white but may be treated in color by most compatible desktop software. For IBM and MAC, art comes on 3 1/2" disks. (5 1/4" available by request–except for IBM volumes 1-4, which come on 5 1/4" disks. 3 1/2" available by request). A hard drive and 640K are required. Accessible through any of the following software programs—MAC: PageMaker ®, ReadySetGo!™ and Quark Xpress ™. Also accessible with Aldus FreeHand ® and Adobe Illustrator ® for modifications.
IBM and Compatibles: PageMaker ®, Ventura Publisher ®, Arts & Letters™, WordPerfect™ 5.0 and 5.1, and others.

YOUTH SPECIALTIES
Call 800/776-8008 to order!

Special offer:
BUY ONE GET
ONE FREE!
ArtSource Vol 1-6 on
IBM or Mac (while
supplies last) Offer #CAC01

Index Use this index to find text items. Use the Image Index beginning on page 349 to find clip art images.

Image Index Use this index to find clip art images.

Use the index beginning on page 347 to find text items.

D

E

M

magazine, 231
magic, 67
magician, 201
magnifying glass, 303
mail, 280, 304
mailbox, 246, 292, 298
maps
   Europe, 303
   Washington, 17
   world, 232, 285, 290
marbled paper, 97
marshmallows, 322
match, 215
medicine, 186
meeting, 182, 191, 225
memo, 194
message, 14, 231
Mexican food, 247
microphone, 69
microscope, 233
"MILK," 306
miner, 177
mirror, 143
money, 123, 249
   "ATM" machine, 272
   dollar bill, 77, 103, 223, 294
   pot of gold, 262
   "RED INK," 193
   shark, 29
monkey, 290
moon, 111, 227, 232
mother and child, 206, 289
motorcycle, 274, 321
Mountie, 242
mouse (animal), 202, 237, 287
mouse (computer), 38
movie
   camera, 185
   film reel, 297
music, 247
   accordion, 264
   cello, 248
   compact disc, 295
   conductor, 214
   cornet, 294
   drum, 63, 225, 247
   fiddle, 223

flute, 63
guitar, 52, 79, 209, 247
jazz trio, 6
microphone, 69
piano, 8, 21, 63, 230, 273
saxophone, 15, 217
sheet music, 298
sound speaker, 91
trumpet, 247, 294

N

nest, 111, 255, 295
newspaper, 200, 245, 250

O

observatory, 247
occupations
   architect, 181
   carpenter, 202
   chef, 192
   daredevil, 181
   doctor, 135, 183, 280
   hairdresser, 206
   magician, 201
   miner, 177
   photographer, 230
   salesman, 226
   scientist, 246
   surgeon, 246
   teacher, 181
office workers, 13, 191, 200, 205, 206,
   207, 225
   cheerleader, 193
   communication, 207
   desktop publisher, 49
   salesman, 226
oil spill, 178
oil well, 171
ornaments, 14, 27, 89, 311, 313, 314
   arabesque, 131, 147, 165, 169,
     170
   historical, 147, 163, 164, 168,
     169
   tiles, 185
ostrich, 174
owl, 143

357

CD-ROM Instructions There are two ways to use the images from the CD-ROM: by importing the files into your software program using its built-in graphics features, or by using the Kudo Catalog Reader to drag and drop the image into software programs such as PageMaker, QuarkXPress, Word, and WordPerfect.

Importing clip art into your software program

Virtually every desktop publishing, graphics, word processing, and presentation software program for Windows includes a feature that allows you to import and manipulate clip art. Each program does it a bit differently, so you will need to refer to your program's User's Guide for the details. Typically, you will find instructions under a heading in the index such as "clip art" or "graphics"— "placing" or "importing."

Once you understand the procedure, you're ready to locate an image on the CD-ROM. First, browse through the Clip Art Catalog (beginning on page 159) and find the image you want to use (the Image Index beginning on page 349 will help you find a particular subject).

Important: The Clip Art Crazy CD-ROM is for use BY THE PURCHASER ONLY. For more information about using the artwork, see page 48.

Beside each image is one or more file names, for example: art_15_b.wmf. The first three letters in the name are an abbreviation of the publisher's name (Art Parts). Next is an underline followed by a two-digit number that corresponds to the listing in the book (15), followed by another underline and a single letter that tells you whether the image is black and white (B) or color (C). In the Aridi chapter the (M) denotes files that include two images, one color and one black and white. In the PhotoDisc directory the (H) denotes a second version of the file in high-resolution. The period is followed by three letters

(BMP, EPS, TIF, WMF) that tell you the type of file it is (file formats are discussed in detail beginning on page 35).

When you are prompted for the location of the file you want to use, choose the letter of your CD-ROM drive, then highlight the "content" directory, the directory of the company that produced the image, and select the file name that corresponds to the image and import it. The path for the example below (from PageMaker 5.0) is:

e:\content\artparts\art_15_b.wmf

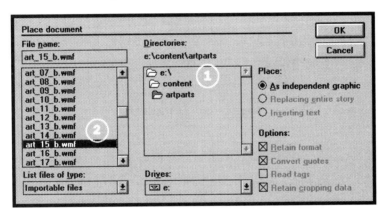

The CD-ROM is loaded in the E: drive and the clip art images are located in the "content" directory. There is a subdirectory for each publisher, in this case the artparts directory (1) is open and the art_15_b.wmf image file (2) is selected. The dialog box for other programs may look a bit different, but selecting the path is the same.

A word about file size

The files on the *Clip Art Crazy CD-ROM* range in size from less than 5000 bytes to over 3,000,000 bytes (3 megabytes [MB]). If you attempt to view, import, or print a large or complex image and get an "out of memory" message, it is likely that you have insufficient system or printer memory to process the image. It may be necessary to upgrade your hardware or software to be able to use images of this size. To see the file size of a particular image, use the Kudo Catalog Reader, the Windows 3.1 File Manager (select View>All File Details), or the Windows 95 Windows Explorer (select View>Details).

Using the Kudo Catalog Reader

You can also access the images by installing the Kudo Catalog Reader. It allows you to browse through the images on the *Clip Art Crazy CD-ROM* on your computer screen and to drag and drop images into versions of applications such as PageMaker, QuarkXPress, Word, and WordPerfect (see the Kudo Catalog Reader Help Menu for a list of compatible programs).

To install the Kudo Catalog Reader:

1. Start Windows and place the *Clip Art Crazy CD-ROM* in your CD-ROM drive.

2. Windows 3.1: Choose Run from the File menu in Program Manager.

    Windows 95: Click the Start button and then click Run.

3. If the *Clip Art Crazy CD-ROM* is in drive D, type:

    D:\WINSTALL.EXE

    If the CD-ROM is in a different drive, substitute the "D" with the correct drive letter.

4. Follow the prompts for installing the Kudo Catalog Reader.

5. Once the catalog reader is installed, you can double-click the lightbulb icons to view thumbnails of the images for each company.

For details on all the features of the Catalog Reader double-click the Kudoread "?" icon or choose Help>Index from the Kudo Image Catalog menu bar.